Grow
Mother's Heart

Devotions of Faith, Hope, and Love from Mothers
PAST, PRESENT, AND FUTURE

Karen Whiting
Proverbs 2:2

Karen Whiting

AMG
PUBLISHERS

Growing a Mother's Heart:
Devotions of Faith, Hope, and Love,
from Mothers Past, Present, and Future
Copyright © 2021 by Karen Whiting

Published by AMG Publishers
6815 Shallowford Road
Chattanooga, Tennessee 37421

ISBN 13: 978-1-61715-560-4
First Printing—March 2021

Cover designed by Brian Wooten, Brikwoo Creative Group, Chattanooga, Tennessee

Editing, interior design, and typesetting by Rick Steele Editorial Services
(https://steeleeditorialservices.myportfolio.com)

Printed in the United States of America

dedicated to...

my daughters and other loved ones who have become moms,
especially:

Rebecca White

Kimberly Whiting

Darlene Pena

Mira Whiting

Brittany Sims

You and all moms make a difference!

Dear Moms,

Being a mother is so special and at the same time messy, crazy, unpredictable, scary, and a roller coaster ride. We all want to be the best mom but can feel like failures when things go wrong. It's all okay and you are good enough if you love your children. Their smiles, kisses, hugs, and cuddles all express their love.

Stories help us learn better than anyone telling us what to do. Real moms, past and present bring us hope, laughter, tears, and joy through sharing their experiences. They remind us that we are okay too. They give us new ideas of what to try with our children (and some show us what not to do).

We have real needs for support, love, assurance, and more and the moms who share in these pages also share what fills their needs. We walk beside one another through the relatable tales of woe and joy.

Our children need us to respond to their needs and understand them and these stories also show us how to do that. The quotes from children remind us that they see life differently and help us take ourselves less seriously.

Even when we make a mistake, we can recover, and our lessons help show our children how we survive and meet challenges. We encourage them through our actions and words to try to do their best and laugh at mistakes and then try again.

I love being with moms of all ages and listening to them. We get each other. We can be ourselves and empathize and laugh together.

Hold onto your faith and trust God to guide you.

Karen

table of contents

Week 1

Treasuring the Gift of Life

Prayer to Grow a Mother's Heart

Father God, you are the Creator. I'm amazed at the child I hug and how you wove the DNA to create such beauty. Each little toe and finger is beautiful. I look into such beautiful eyes and wonder what my child sees and thinks. From the first moment I have wondered, what will my baby see in me? Will I measure up and meet my little child's needs? I want to be a great mother, but every day and every challenge are new to me. A tiny babe is so fragile, and at every age the heart is delicate.

People look to see my eyes, nose, or hands in my child or those of my husband or another family member. There's such joy in watching a squirming, little face, eyes that see things for the very first time, and that wonder continues as my child grows and discovers the world. What a miracle to see life in my child and to watch this precious one grow. I never knew I could feel such delight and yet feel so tired.

Please help me grow a mother's heart and help me to love my child unconditionally. Help me to remember the early days and all the joys of motherhood. Help me face the challenges with faith.

Wisdom from Future Moms

Mommy tuck me in, so I feel like I'm stuffed in a soft taco shell.

Mom is like my heart because she's that close to me.

When the baby falls out of your tummy can I give her a bottle?

A Treasured Kiss

And He went down with them and came to Nazareth, and He continued in subjection to them; and His mother treasured all these things in her heart. LUKE 2:51

One morning Karen kissed her young son, then watched him turn, wipe off the kiss, and pat his chest. She felt sad, thinking he was growing up and feeling too old for kisses. Suddenly, he twirled around, looked up, and said, "Do you know what I did?" She shook her head no, not wanting to admit that she noticed he brushed off the kiss.

Grinning, he said, "I took the kiss you gave me and put it in my heart. If I get sad or mad today, I'll be okay 'cause it will be here where I can feel it. I can take it out if I need it." His words lifted her heart. Karen's son treasured the kiss and wanted to keep it close to him all day.

Her kiss gave her son who struggled with anger and anxiety encouragement. It made her day. She also recalled when her older daughter had jumped on the bed and squeezed herself in between her husband and herself and said, "Now I feel loved." Treasured memories to store.

> ### Today's Mom Step
> Store up a memory today of something your child did and store up a scripture too.

A mother's kisses and hugs mean so much to little ones from healing a hurting heart, the kiss on a cut, or cuddling up when a child's afraid. We see the power of a mother's love in kisses and hugs. Hugs should always be given freely at all ages. As children grow, our encouraging words also embrace them with love and strengthen them to face problems they encounter.

Moms collect precious memories: a child's first steps, unexpected words said, a weed picked as a gift, and little kisses and hugs stored in their hearts. We speak about them with family and friends. If we have time, we post or journal about those moments. The God who loves us shares our joy of each precious memory. A stored-up bounty of priceless treasure can refresh our hearts at any time.

Treasured Thoughts (Biblical Mom, Mary, Mother of Jesus)

But Mary treasured all these things, pondering them in her heart.
LUKE 2:19

His name Emanuel means 'God saves." Jesus is the name most known of all names in the Bible. His mother Mary is the most-often-mentioned mother in the Bible. The New Testament opens with news of the birth of Jesus, the promised Messiah. He has many names.

God chose Mary to be the mother of Jesus. She was too young, unmarried, and from a small town. In a flash the angel Gabriel appeared to her and said, "Do not be afraid." Every time an angel appears in the Bible the first words are, "Do not fear." The angel explained God's request for her to have this baby. She asked, "How can this happen? I'm a virgin." Gabriel explained that God would take care of it for God who made the universe and breathed life into dust to make man could do the impossible. God's Holy Spirit would bring about the conception.

Wow! Life from dust, and now life direct from God the life-giver. Each baby you treasure owes his or her life to God. How did you feel when you first suspected you were pregnant? Or when you first received news you would be a mom through adoption? What thoughts filled your mind? What did you think when you first wrapped your arms around your child? Did your mind fill with wonder at words spoken about your child? Do you treasure and reflect on those words?

Today's Mom Step

Close your eyes and remember the first moments with your child.

Mary and her husband, Joseph, the man she married after she became pregnant, brought Jesus to the Temple. This followed the Jewish custom. There Mary heard prophecies about her son Jesus. He would be the light to unbelievers. Simeon, an old man thanked God for the child, and said he had seen God's salvation. Mary did not understand, but she treasured the words and pondered them.

Little Dents

But now, O Lord You are our Father, we are the clay, and You our potter; and all of us are the work of Your hand. ISAIAH 64:8 NIV

On vacation, Teresa's family toured a glass factory. It fascinated her daughter Rebecca to see colors swirl out, as workers blew on multi-colored glass and formed each piece into a unique shape. Her husband took Rebecca to shop while Teresa tended their younger children.

Later, Rebecca anxiously said, "Daddy bought you a pretty present for your birthday, even though it has a few dents in it. The colors are pretty, Mom, so don't be upset when you open it." How special to have our children be concerned about our feelings!

A few days later, Teresa smiled when she unwrapped the gift: an expensive vase with three carefully crafted indentations. It took gentle but firm pressure to create the dents without breaking the vase.

The vase is a valuable treasure to those who understand the care and skill involved. Sometimes God's plans seem like ugly unwanted dents until we step back and see His care and skill in creating dents and learn to value the beauty of His handiwork.

When we think of our own imperfections or those of our children, think how God carefully formed those little dents. He loves us just the way He created us. He wants us to realize that He gave us life and shapes us with purpose. He molded the DNA together.

> **Today's Mom Step**
>
> Treasure your child and thank God for the way He created your child.

Whether a dent is original or formed by a cave in from pressures, because we are made of moldable clay, not steel, we can give thanks that we are not perfect and praise God because He is perfect. We can look at our children and smile with amazement at how God created every hair and cell and know He treasures our children, including what we perceive as perfections and flaws.

Abigail Snelling: A Life Worth Living (Historic Mom)

I have fought the good fight, I have finished the course, I have kept the faith. 2 TIMOTHY 4:7

We want to make a difference and live a life worth living. That's what we want for our children from the moment we hold each one. Abigail Snelling lived life well amid great hardships. She forged the way for women in military families. Born shortly after the American Revolution, in 1797, at six weeks old, her family moved from Boston to Michigan. Highlights of her life include:

1. She lived at Fort Bellefonte, when frontier explorers Lewis and Clark visited. Her parents died from fever at the fort, leaving her at age twelve, and her siblings orphaned.

2. She visited with future president William Henry Harrison on one of her trips.

3. Lived with grandparents in Boston for three years. At age fifteen she moved to Detroit, lived with her oldest brother, then soon married army Captain Josiah Snelling.

4. Filled powder bags for cannons two hours after her wedding as her husband fought and lost a battle to the British in the War of 1812. He was captured, so she went to Boston and gave birth to their first child, who graduated from West Point when he grew up.

5. Moved several more times including to establish Fort Snelling in Minnesota. There she taught school and shared her faith in leading Sunday School for children in the fort. She also planned picnics, parties, and celebrations, and assisted local families and native Americans.

6. Widowed at age twenty-one, she spent years applying for her husband's pension. Her persistence opened doors for widows to receive pensions. She outlived a second husband, ran a boarding house, and in her older years lived on a farm with her son.

> **Today's Mom Step**
> Live your life; let challenges make you stronger and stay in touch with your network.

Abigail persisted and made a difference in many lives. Her biggest key to success came from a large network of family and friends. Faith and connections brought her strength. She wrote letters continually to stay in touch. Deep relationships make a big difference

Every Life Is Precious

For I know the plans that I have for you,' declares the Lord, 'plans for welfare and not for calamity to give you a future and a hope.
JEREMIAH 29:11

Linda's eighteen-month-old baby, Laura, lay in a hospital bed in a coma after a violent car crash. Doctors urged Linda to disconnect the tubes and let Laura die, but she prayed. Her little girls' life remained in God's hands. She had recently discovered she was pregnant, and the growing life in her encouraged Linda to trust God. A year later when Linda placed her newborn son in Laura's arms, her precious daughter opened her eyes.

Although handicapped, Laura enjoyed life. Laura could not speak with her voice, but she communicated through smiles, blinking, and eye movements. She enjoyed having her mom move her wheelchair to music. She loved books like the Chronicles of Narnia, Adventures in Odyssey radio drama, and baking cookies for her family and friends. She sponsored and wrote to three children in the Compassion International program. She also shared how she met Jesus in heaven while still in a coma. After thirty years, she went home to the Lord, and Linda knows that her precious daughter Laura is dancing in heaven.

After the accident, Linda Evans Shepherd started writing, started a prayer ministry, a ministry to help suicidal people, and a ministry for women who speak and write. She also advocates for the injured and disabled. Prayer is her faithful companion in all circumstances. She's always reaching out with new ideas to touch people, bring hope, and share the bond of motherhood. Linda says, "I raised a handicapped daughter I loved, but really, don't we all have special needs? We loved Laura not because of what she could achieve but because she was God's gift to her family."

> **Today's Mom Step**
>
> Spend time with your children, enjoy each smile, and thank God for their precious lives.

Week 2

It's a Brand New Day!

Prayer to Face Each Day

Dear Lord, thank you for blessing me with children. The sleepless nights, endless work, and heartaches are all worth it when my child smiles or hugs me. The messiness, muddy footprints, and smudged handprints on the wall are all signs of my little one leaving their mark. The sounds of their voices make me laugh while their cries pierce my heart.

Help me in the daily struggle to make wise decisions and show my love while guiding their steps and helping them mature. Help me share my faith, so they might trust in you.

Give me strength each day to face the challenges. Help me overcome piles of laundry and dishes. Let me relax enough to enjoy my children as I read to them, share conversations, and tuck them in bed. As they grow, let our relationships grow, and help us stay connected with love.

Thank you for guiding me and being an example of how to love my children as you love me. Let me face each brand-new day with a sense of adventure and joy as I watch my children explore and discover more of the world around them.

Wisdom from Future Moms

I know it's a bad day when mom keeps taking breaks to pray. That happens when I break something or make a huge mess.

Mom says I need to brush my teeth in the morning so I will smell sweet and remember to say sweet words and not whine.

Morning Larks and Night Owls

They [God's mercies, loving kindnesses, compassion] are new every morning; Great is Your faithfulness. LAMENTATIONS 3:23

Karen is not a morning person. She prayed her children would not wake early. However, her first child, Rebecca, was a morning lark. Many mornings, she woke up energized and ready to face the day. She raced to her mom's room, tugged the cord to pull the drapes open, and cheerfully sang out, "Mom! It's a brand-new day."

Karen tried to open her eyelids. She'd ask, "Are your brothers awake?"

If Rebecca said yes, Karen responded, "Can you make sure they are playing or give them some breakfast?"

Rebecca raced off to check on the other children and give her mother a few minutes to wake up. If the other children were not awake, Karen invited Rebecca to join her in bed and cuddle with her. Daddy always left for work before anyone else was up. Rebecca jumped in and chattered about the adventures of a new day.

Some mornings are hard to face while, others bring joy because of special activities planned. For little ones, every day brings something new as they discover the world around them. Karen realized she could start slowly while listening to happy sounds and sitting where she could watch her children eat and play. She used the time to praise God while coming up with a few reasons to be grateful. If she had a hard time coming up with grateful thoughts, she'd ask her children to call

> ### Today's Mom Step
> Whatever part of the day is hardest, pause to sit back and view life through your child's eyes and thank God for your blessings and new adventures.

out praises and happy thoughts. That routine energized her and inspired her to move forward each day with fresh faith and a child's perspective. Then she could call out, "This is the day that God has made. Let us rejoice."

The First Birth (Biblical Mom, Eve)

Now the man had relations with his wife Eve, and she conceived and gave birth to Cain, and she said, "I have gotten a manchild with the help of the Lord." GENESIS 4:1

A little man, the first infant ever. Imagine Eve's wonder and amazement. She probably saw animals give birth but never saw a human infant before Cain. Most women want their mother or another woman around when they give birth, but Eve did not have that option. The one parent she knew, the Lord, helped her, and she appreciated it.

The first smile, step, and word that came rocked her world. Each new day of Cain's life brought new wonder. She had no expectation of when to anticipate each first. She faced no comparisons to other children and their moms. Eve and Adam could simply rejoice with everything Cain experienced.

After being cast out of the Garden of Eden, the perfect garden, we learn about two events. We learn of the intimacy between Adam and Eve and the birth of Cain, the first infant. There's no mention of the labor of growing and cooking food or building a home. There's no mention of labor pains that God spoke about in Genesis 3:16 after Eve and Adam ate the forbidden fruit. But we can see from scripture that, like today, nothing was more important than starting a family and bringing a new life into the world. Holding our new baby still overshadows the pain of labor. The birth of Cain likely became their most wonderful day after leaving Eden.

Troubles melt away as we hold our newborn babies. Holding a new life remains a precious memory that holds great promise. Each first is precious and a reminder of God's love and creative abilities.

Today's Mom Step

Share with each child the joy and love you felt the first time you saw his or her face.

After the Storm

And He [Jesus] got up and rebuked the wind and said to the sea, "Hush, be still." And the wind died down and it became perfectly calm. MARK 4:39

Whoosh! Crash! Banging sounds filled the air throughout the night, as Karen and her children slept off and on through the biggest storm that she had even experienced. Meteorologists expected the storm to be further away but now declared that people in certain areas needed to stay home rather than attempt to evacuate, including Karen's home area. They had prepared as best they could with her husband away on military orders.

During the night, they prayed and read the Bible in the large closet where they stayed. Finally, Karen read about Jesus calming the storm, and prayed with her five children for God to stop the winds. Everything became quiet. The storm ceased. Her son Michael yelled, "You should have read that one first, Mom!" Laughter filled the closet.

Karen ventured out with her oldest children as the sun shone that morning. Water covered the first floor, along with broken glass from windows and fallen pictures. Outside broken pieces of orange roof tiles lay everywhere. Neighbors emerged from their homes to look around and find out how everyone survived. Karen's house stood although damaged while everyone remained safe. Tweets and chirps of birds filled the air mixed with unusual bird sounds. Exotic birds in nearby trees that had escaped from the zoo celebrated the new day filled with sunshine and a bright blue sky.

Karen and her children thanked God for safety and asked for guidance in the adventure of restoring their home. They bailed water out of the sunken living room,

> **Today's Mom Step**
> Live your life; let challenges make you stronger and stay in touch with your network.

moved outside furniture back to the porch, and picked up broken glass and pictures that had crashed on the floor.

Anna Jarvis, Founder of Mother's Day (Historic Mom)

"Her children rise up and bless her; Her husband also, and he praises her . . ." PROVERBS 31:27

Anna Jarvis, a woman who never married and never gave birth to children, struggled to celebrate her own mother and other mothers with a special day to honor their contributions. She succeeded where others had failed, and used the carnation, her mother's favorite flower, as a symbol of a mother's pure love. What a legacy she gave her mother that reflects their bond of love.

In England, starting in the 1600s, churches celebrated Mothering Sunday on the fourth Sunday of Lent to honor Mary and all mothers. They held a prayer service, and children gave flowers and little gifts to their mothers.

Julia Ward Howe, a mother of six and author of "The Battle Hymn of the Republic," championed June second as a day to honor mothers. She held a meeting in Boston for several years, but it never caught on because of her political and negative focus.

Anna, inspired by her late mother's desire to honor and value mothers, gathered friends who wrote letters to people in power and lobbied for several years. In 1914, President Woodrow Wilson signed a resolution designating the second Sunday of May as Mother's Day. That brand-new holiday for mothers began May 8, 1914. It's the most popular day of the year for phone calls around the world. Mothers love to hear the voices of their children. The first sound a baby often makes is "ma." The day is also the busiest day of the year for restaurants. Nothing touches a mother's heart quite like hugs and children's expressions of their love or the calls from grown children who have moved further away.

Knit Together

You formed my inward parts; You knit me together in my mother's womb. PSALM 139:13

Kerry started knitting as a young girl. By her teens she knitted fancy sweaters with intricate Irish knit patterns and others with bright colored designs. She also learned to weave, crochet, sew, and sculpt. Forming something and seeing it take shape fascinated her.

When Kerry married and became pregnant, she and her husband thanked God. She studied Psalm 139 and the wonder of God forming each new life inside a mother's womb. Kerry recognized that He knit and molded DNA instead of strings of yarn. Soon, Kerry took a pottery class to work with clay, and this experience caused her to reflect on how this baby grew inside her. She knew God was skillfully forming every cell, organ, and body part.

As she felt kicks and flutters, she smiled and shared those feelings with her husband. One day she gave a little scream and landed on the floor. Her husband asked, "What happened?"

Kerry replied, "The baby kicked so hard that he kicked me off the chair." The day finally came with twinges of pain followed by contractions and pushing. She struggled with hard work and pain she had not experienced before that morning. Finally, she heard the cry of her son. The doctor put him on her chest, and she touched him, and looked at him for the first time.

Like any mother, Kerry checked fingers, toes, eyes, and nose. What a perfect baby boy! All the months of waiting and wondering how her child would look, feel, and smell become reality. All the pain of the pregnancy and birth lay behind. She knew he had a strong kick and that he actually pushed himself over in his hospital bassinet did not surprise her, although it frustrated and surprised the nurses. God's ability to create surpassed anything she could ever make.

> **Today's Mom Step**
>
> When you make something remember to thank God for forming your child.

Week 3

Choose Joy!

Prayer for Joy

Lord, I have chosen to follow you, my source of hope. Help me look back to see how you have brought me through my past and remained faithful to me. That fills my heart with gratitude.

Help me look up to trust you and not my problems. I can't do life alone, so thanks for coming along side me and for providing loved ones in my life to walk with me. You give me hope and strength to face the days ahead. Let me look beyond my earthly life to believe in the joys of heaven. Help me to hold onto joy in my soul, the joy of knowing how much you love me and the ones I love.

Guide me to be adaptable and find blessings in the midst of struggles and hassles. Help me find a reason to rejoice each day and a "mom moment" to treasure. Guide me to reach out to You, loved ones, and friends to praise You. Let us remind one another of the blessings of love that bring joy every day. Let me sprinkle joy into my children's lives and praise you with them.

Wisdom from Future Moms

Mothers should spend their time dancing with their children so they will always be happy.

Mom can be silly too. She plays Mario cards with me.

Turn around Birthday Tears

Anxiety in a man's heart weighs it down, but a good word makes it glad. PROVERBS 12:25

Becky held such high expectations for her birthday that it seemed no matter what her mom planned, at some point she erupted in tears. At last her mother decided she must feel too overwhelmed with so much happening. She chose to do one thing each hour for Becky and make party time a little lighter. They paused after each little activity to thank God for the blessings and to choose joy. Each time Rebecca said, "I'm happy it's my birthday."

They started the morning with a birthday fruit bowl and one present to open. Each hour a sibling would yell "SURPRISE!!!" compliment Rebecca, and then present her with a little gift or an activity. Her dad would then snap a photo, and they'd chat about a caption to write for the photo.

Some hours after opening a gift from a relative, she'd call the person and then write a thank you note. She kept busy so she didn't build up more expectations. When friends showed up, they kept things simple with a few games. Becky gave each guest a bookmark to fill in with games played to remember the day. They played a musical chair type game with Becky in the center and the person who was out then gave her a gift to open. Being out became fun too. Once the gift was opened, the ones left would continue the game and sat with Becky.

After games, cupcakes with fruit and clown ice cream cones already prepared made passing out food simple. Everyone sang "Happy Birthday," and her mom served the

---

Today's Mom Step

Avoid feeling overwhelmed by choosing to focus on one thing at a time; break big problems or celebrations into smaller bites, and choose joy.

---

guests at one time. After eating, the children enjoyed some free play time. Becky passed out a gift bag to each guest as they left. Needless to say, she thoroughly enjoyed her day!

Rainy, Noisy Days and Nights
(Biblical Mom, Noah's Wife)

I set My bow in the cloud, and it shall be for a sign of a covenant between Me and the earth. GENESIS 9:13

Imagine living in a floating zoo for forty rainy days plus another eighty days. The noise, smell, and ruckus would outdo any home, not to mention the dark skies and lack of sunshine making things gloomy. That's where God sent Noah and his family. It took one hundred years for Noah and his sons to build the ark. *These men must have had very patient wives.* It also gave the four women time to adjust to the idea of a flood.

The Bible never mentions names Noah's wife or the other three women. Moms sometimes lose their names and become so and so's mom or wife. Hebrew tradition calls Noah's wife *Naamah*. That means sweet or pleasant. It also means beauty or grace. We never hear a peep out of her. She and the other women remained silent person as they climbed in and out of the ark.

She stayed by her man and sons for hundreds of years. God commended Noah for pleasing Him. God declared He would destroy all the wickedness in the world. So, Noah's wife and family must not have been wicked. Traveling with eight pleasant family members makes a long trip easier.

Noah's wife remains one of the first people to witness a beautiful rainbow in the sky. She saw a great change from rainy days to a huge colorful arc that God painted in the sky. With no pollution or fog, nothing kept the full colors from sparkling. What a joyful sight to experience as a family. With it came a comforting promise that God would never send a flood to destroy the entire earth again. We can almost hear the women sigh and see tears of joy thinking they had lasted through the tough times and found beauty at the end.

Joy-spiration Time

This is the day which the LORD has made; Let us rejoice and be glad in it. PSALM 118:25

The grumbling, yelling, and screaming noises escalated. Elizabeth had enough. She sang out, "It's Joy-spiration time."

The children yelled back, "It's Joy-spiration time."

They gathered together in the living room with their Bibles ready to focus on God and their blessings. Everyone took a deep breath. They giggled as they slowly let out their breaths.

Elizabeth asked, "What day is this?" Her children responded, "The day the Lord made." Then she asked, "What should we do today?" They answered, "Rejoice and be glad."

"Okay. Let's do it."

Each one stated a praise and a blessing they had experienced. Then they sang a song. They repeated this pattern for a little while, and then Elizabeth asked one of her children to read a Bible passage. They chatted about the Bible story they had read and then sang another song.

After sharing a number of scripture passages, chatting, and singing, Elizabeth said, "I like this noise much better than the grumbles I heard earlier." Everyone smiled and nodded. "So, one at a time, let me know what we can do to make the day better."

She listened to anyone who had a problem, and then they discussed ideas on how to overcome it and how to find joy instead of reasons to grumble. Elizabeth ended the time with a prayer and a group hug. Next, everyone headed to the kitchen for a snack before returning to his or her schoolwork, chores, or play.

Today's Mom Step

When grumbles pop up, turn the day around with gratitude and praise.

As a mom of five, Elizabeth found that taking time to choose joy over grumbles made a huge difference. It also helped her feel more joyful and grateful.

The Joy Lady, Barbara Johnson (Historic Mom)

A joyful heart is good medicine, but a broken spirit dries up the bones. PROVERBS 17:22

Some days we want to turn in our mom badges. Toilets overflow; children break a favorite keepsake, and grape juice spills all over the table and floor. Most of the time we can laugh about the problems on another day. One woman who many moms admired chose joy in the worst scenarios of life. A mother of four, humorist, popular speaker and author, Barbara Johnson always trusted God and looked for blessings around her.

After doctors stated her husband would never be healed from a severe accident, Barbara and her teen sons kept praying. A year later Bill returned to work, fully restored. How they rejoiced!

Barbara and Bill raised four sons and experienced the loss of two of them, one during the Vietnam War and one killed by a drunk driver. She experienced years of alienation from one son who walked away from God along with the joy of his return to follow Christ.

Barbara's faith kept her going as did her joy box. She filled a shoebox with little mementos that gave her joy. It included a joke book from when her boys were little. She continued to collect items, including lots of jokes. Her box overflowed into a joy room.

As a mother, Barbara reached out to other mothers. She started a ministry and gave encouragement to many parents with her words such as, "Live for today, but hold your hands open to tomorrow. Anticipate the future and its changes with joy. There is a seed of God's love in every event, every unpleasant situation in which you may find yourself."

Today's Mom Step

Choose to trust God and find joy, in spite of the circumstances.

There are days when we wonder if we can smile again. Those are days to trust God and know and reflect on Barbara describing tears as being crystalized jewels to God.

Real Love, Real Joy

A gentle answer turns away wrath, but a harsh word stirs up anger.
PROVERBS 15:1

Often, if we are raised in chaos and abuse, like Pam Farrel, our anger and volume escalate. One day, as Pam drove her sons to school, she listened to a Christian radio program dealing with "Mommy anger." Back home, she grabbed her mail; inside her favorite magazine was an article on "Mommy anger." She flipped on the TV, and the talk show host had a panel chatting about "Mommy Anger." Then she picked up her three sons and headed home to focus on homework and cleaning their rooms. Her three sons were ages 3 years old to 12 years old.

They had a rule, "Do not yell up and down the stairs. Show respect and honor and walk to the person and use your "inside voice." Of course, the boys eventually started yelling up and down the stairs. It ignited an old pattern in Pam, so she stood at the bottom step and screamed, "You boys know the rule! If you want something, come down and ask me without yelling!" Her littlest son, sitting at her feet, reached up and tugged her skirt. "Mommy, I don't think Jesus likes it when you yell at us." Zing! Convicted of her bad behavior, she quickly apologized. Soon after, she and her rambunctious sons began to whisper to each other, A gentle answer turns away wrath, but a harsh word stirs up anger.

God had her dig deeper to realize fear of failure triggered her anger. God continued to teach her to manage her emotions. For example, in her public speaking, Pam is known for sharing this story and others with the phrase, "Choose Joy!" In the New Testament, you'll find *chairó* or joy/rejoice more than 70 times. Her favorite definition of joy is "Calm

> **Today's Mom Step**
> (1) writing a few positive statements or scriptures you can recite repetitively that encourage you to focus on the blessings of your children
> (2) making a "Joy Moments" list for yourself and one for each child. (I keep a "Joy Moments" list of things I know create joy.)

Delight." When your stress rises, pause and pray, "God, what would calm this situation, calm me, can calm my child? Lord, what would be a delightful distraction or experience for my child, me and our family?"

Week 4
HUGS (Hope,
Understanding, Guidance,
and Security)

Prayer to Wrap My Children in Love

Lord help me surround my child with HUGS daily:

Let me give Hugs of Hope with sharing faith and helping my little one trust you. Let me be a living example of faith by following you always.

Help me provide HUGS of understanding by pausing to listen before responding. Give me an understanding heart and help me notice my child's needs, personality, and interests to build strong bonds.

Give me wisdom to bless my child with HUGS of guidance to teach my child to choose wisely in life, for I know you have plans to prosper and not harm my child, plans that will provide a future and a hope.

Help me keep my precious child safe to feel secure and loved.

I want to always wrap my arm around my child and say, "I love you." Help me do that with words of encouragement, the guidance of good rules, and the compassion or understanding.

Thank you for blessing me with this precious life and the gift of motherhood. Thank you for the hugs you give with your words and for surrounding me with your love.

Wisdom from Future Moms

To make mom happy, I would clean the house perfectly in one day. Mommy only gives me twenty minutes to clean. I will give my children at least thirty minutes.

Oh no, I forgot something . . . to give you a hug.

The Broken Window

Make your ear attentive to wisdom, incline your heart to understanding. PROVERBS 2:2

"I didn't break Grandma's window. We just played croquet. I do bad things, but I don't lie."

Karen looked at her son and said, "Let's take a walk." She walked with Michael to the back stairs that led to the cellar door. She asked, "Did you go down these stairs?"

Michael nodded and said, "My ball rolled down the steps. I ran down and picked it up and ran right back up."

Karen rolled the ball, handed her son the croquet mallet, and said, "Go pick up the ball and bring it to me. She watched Michael run to the ball. He picked it up, turned around, tossed the mallet over his shoulder, and ran back with the ball.

"I think I know what happened. When you pick up the ball and turn around, you lift the mallet over your shoulder. If you did that at the bottom of the stairs, the mallet would hit the window and break the glass. In science that's called law of motion: an action causes an equal and opposite reaction."

Michael put down the mallet and said, "I didn't know that would happen. I didn't mean to break anything." He turned to his grandma and said, "I'm sorry Grandma. I can do chores to pay for the window."

Today's Mom Step Investigate problems so you can show understanding and give the right guidance.

Grandma hugged Michael and said, "Now I know it was an accident. I understand and forgive you."

Michael said, "I will look before I put the mallet over my shoulder. I don't want to hit anyone or break anything else."

Sarah's Long-Awaited Hug (Biblical Mom)

Behold, children are a gift of the LORD, *the fruit of the womb is a reward.* PSALM 127:3

Sarah's name means princess. Abraham, her husband, mentioned her great beauty in Genesis 12:11. God blessed Abraham with great wealth. Yes, she had looks, money, and a husband who loved her, but she longed for a baby.

Year after year, Sarah remained infertile with no life inside her. When at last three visitors came and promised that in one year, she would have a son, she laughed. She thought, "After I am worn out, and my lord is old, shall I have pleasure?"

She became pregnant, felt her baby move and kick inside her, and gave birth to the promised son. At last, they held their little boy, and Abraham named him Isaac. Isaac means laughter. In Genesis 21:6 Sarah expresses her joy, "God has made laughter for me; everyone who hears will laugh with me." Sarah nursed him, and Abraham held a great feast when Sarah weaned him. They rejoiced and showered Isaac with love.

Sarah moved with her husband when he took them from their homeland and journeyed through the desert to an unknown land, following God's call. In Hebrews 11:11, we read that Sarah trusted God and put her faith in Him.

Sarah died before Isaac married. When Isaac married his wife Rebekah, we learn that his wife comforted him on the loss of his mother. He must have loved his mother and missed her. Like his parents, Isaac and his wife also experienced infertility and then, after praying, the blessings of

> **Today's Mom Step**
> Thank God for the gift of your child.

children. Sarah would have hugged and nurtured her son every day because she knew he was a precious gift from God.

Hug of Mercy

Yet for this reason I found mercy, so that in me as the foremost, Jesus Christ might demonstrate His perfect patience as an example for those who would believe in Him for eternal life. 1 TIMOTHY 1:16

A cake and pretty decorations sat on the table, ready for a party.

"Mommy. Mommy, I'm sorry I fell asleep without cleaning up. The table looks pretty now. Will it be like the book about the little red hen, the book on the table? No work, so no party?"

Julia smiled at her daughter and said, "We'll see." Her son came in and said almost the same thing and she told him, "We'll see."

Then her older daughter Kate rushed in and said, "Mom, I'm sorry. I got busy talking to Jenny on the phone and didn't make anyone clean up. Will I be left out of the party?"

Julia smiled again and said, "Let me get dressed and then we'll talk."

Julia sat at the table and invited her children to sit. She said, "I came home last night to a big mess. Laundry baskets filled with unfolded clothes, dirty dishes everywhere, and I'm sure you know what toys and things you didn't put away." They nodded.

"I felt angry and wanted to give everyone extra chores. Then I prayed. I remembered God forgave me and showed me mercy. I didn't deserve to be forgiven, including for my anger last night. I chose to show mercy to all of you. We'll enjoy it later after your schoolwork."

> **Today's Mom Step**
> Show mercy to help your children understand God's mercy.

Everyone yelled, "Thanks mommy!"

Kate said, "We don't deserve the party, but we are grateful." She turned to her brother and sister and said, "Let's show mom we are thankful by doing our work." After they completed their work, they ate cake and played games.

A Mother's HUGS Make a Difference (Historic Mom)

Train up a child in the way he should go, even when he is old he will not depart from it. PROVERBS 22:6

The great inventor Thomas Edison, said, "My mother was the making of me. She was so true, so sure of me; and I felt I had something to live for, someone I must not disappoint." Neighbors saw Nancy as a caring friend who often baked goodies for the local children. A mother is a child's first teacher.

Thomas' constant questions frustrated teachers, so formal schooling had only lasted three months. Nancy Elliot Edison, the daughter of an American Revolutionary War hero, homeschooled him once he left school. As a faithful follower of God, Nancy had received training to be a teacher. She used that training to teach him reading, writing, and arithmetic. Nancy realized he learned to read almost by himself. She taught him on their porch, where she set rules and he worked hard, although he never did well in math. She and her husband encouraged his reading. He set up a laboratory in the basement after he read *Parker's School Philosophy* that inspired him to become a scientist. Newspaper articles on electricity drew him to study that too. His mother helped him apply for a job to sell newspapers so he could buy more supplies for his experiments.

Thomas was her seventh child, but three of his siblings died before his first birthday and two had left home. He didn't start talking until age four, possibly due to hearing loss from scarlet fever, but his mother always believed in his intelligence. She never gave up on her son and gave him the HUGS of hope, understanding, guidance, and the security of her love. When she felt she had taught him all she knew, she encouraged him to read books from the library, and he did.

Today's Mom Step

Nurture your child's curiosity and provide each one with materials that match interests.

Nancy gave Thomas the HUGS he needed to succeed in life.

HUGS of Joy

For we are His workmanship, created in Christ Jesus for good works, which God prepared beforehand so that we would walk in them. EPHESIANS 2:10

Alpaca pillows, alarm clocks, animals, apples, angels, airplanes, anchors, an anthology, atlas, Almond Joy® bars, and more, covered the table. A cake in the kitchen shaped with the letter "A" would add to the celebration. Kim planned to surprise her teens since both had earned straight A's. Grandma arrived before Michael and the kids came home from watching a movie.

Everyone received a pad and pen to see if they could identify all the objects. Some of them came up with creative ideas for naming objects, like labeling something as an awesome object, ambiguous item, or additional stuff received giggles and applause for amazing thinking. She snapped photos to capture the memory. They enjoyed receiving new "A" items to add to their rooms as momentous of the celebration. They laughed as they ate the cake, and Grandma gave them each a little gift bag.

Kim's daughter smiled and said, "I didn't expect any of this. It's fun."

Grandma recalled times she simply surprised her family for little reasons and sometimes just to say, "We love you." Unexpected celebrations of approval and hard work sprinkles joy in family life and adds special memory hugs.

Noticing someone worked hard on a project, learned to tie a shoe, mow the lawn, catch a ball, drive a car, or master fractions can be encouraged with little moments of fun that also fills the home with joy. A special dessert, meal out, a movie night, or other surprise, all express, "We're proud of you and your efforts! Good job!"

Today's Mom Step

Celebrate little successes, as that gives children hope and encouragement.

Week 5

How Can My Children Be

So Wise?

Prayer for Wisdom

Father, thank you for giving my child a heart filled with love and the wisdom of a child. Weeds that look pretty to a child, along with rocks, bugs, leaves, and other natural items that fascinate my little one, become gifts of love for me. More than the items, all the smiles, wonder found in life, and hugs, are precious memories. Let me rejoice in tiny marvels God created and help me see the world as my child sees it.

Cuddles and snuggles of finding comfort in me is another gift that reminds me how my child responds to love. Blowing kisses and happy waves when we part and running feet to greet me when we reunite are gifts that fill my heart when plans pull us apart.

Help me to rejoice in gifts of love and be thankful in coming days as my child grows up as days of childhood quickly pass. Let those memories be a treasure that lasts.

As I listen to my child and hear innocent wisdom, let me rejoice in how their minds work and how they see the world.

Wisdom from Future Moms

The hardest thing for mom is to make me do my schoolwork. If I were a mother, I would give my children lots of candy to get them to work.

When I'm a mom I will get my kids cute clothes.

Dandy Lions

Like apples of gold in settings of silver is a word spoken in right circumstances. PROVERBS 25:11

Michael held out a bunch of yellow blossoms to his mom and said, "Purty flowers, purty mommy."

"Thank you so much, Michael. Your gift and words make me smile. That made my day." Mommy said, then she hugged him and took his gift. She added, "These are called dandelions."

Michael shook his head and said, "No roar. Not lions, flowers."

Mommy laughed, "That's the name of the flower. It is a funny thing to call a flower."

Mommy said, "Let's have fun with these flowers. Some people call them weeds." She got some white circle-shaped stickers and colored pencils. She drew a face on one and stuck it in the middle of one yellow dandelion. "Now you can see how the flower looks like the mane of a lion."

Michael drew eyes and mouths on the circles and pressed them onto the flowers. All day long, he walked back to the little vase of dandelions, and said, "Funny lions," and giggled.

They took a walk, and Michael pointed out all the little funny lions dotting the lawns. They looked at the fuzzy white balls that came from the dandelions. Mommy said, "It's easy to blow on the fuzzy balls, and that spreads the seeds for more dandelions to grow. Michael blew on one and called them, "Blow balls."

Today's Mom Step

Take time to enjoy little gifts of hugs and wildflowers from your children and laugh together at funny names in nature.

GROWING A MOTHER'S HEART

Mommy pointed out other funny names in nature like the Dogwood tree, babbling brook, and tadpoles in the pond. Michael laughed and barked at trees being called dogs; he imitated the sounds of the brook, and he pointed out the fast-swimming poles.

Reuben's Gift to His Mom Leah (Biblical Mom)

Now in the days of wheat harvest Reuben went and found mandrakes in the field, and brought them to his mother Leah. Then Rachel said to Leah, "Please give me some of your son's mandrakes." GENESIS 30:14

Reuben found mandrakes, a medicinal plant, and gave them to his mother Leah. Leah's husband, Jacob, never wanted to marry her. He worked seven years for her father for a promise of marriage, but not to Leah. He wanted her sister, but her father tricked him into marrying Leah first. Jacob worked seven more years to finally marry Leah's gorgeous sister Rachel. Unloved by her husband, Leah had six sons and one daughter. This son showed love with his gift of a treasured plant.

However, Rachel, not satisfied with beauty and her husband's love, wanted what little Leah possessed. She wanted those mandrakes. Rachel had no children and felt jealous of Leah's motherhood. They had huge sister problems. Leah named her sons to get her husband's attention. *Reuben* means, "Behold a son." She wanted Jacob to notice she gave him a son. Her second son's name, *Simeon,* means "hearing," because she believed God heard her cries of being unloved. The third son, *Levi,* means "joined" in hopes another child would draw her husband close to her. With her fourth son, she gave up hoping for Jacob's love and named him *Judah,* meaning "Let God be praised." She finally realized she could be satisfied with the love of God and her sons.

Hopefully, your husband loves and cherishes you. God always loves you, and that's a forever love. God gave Leah a gift of many children, including Judah, the ancestor of Jesus. Our children, our most precious gifts from God, respond to our mother's love and they show that with little gifts they give you.

Today's Mom Step

Rejoice with gifts from your children and know that each one comes from the heart.

Rocky Family

You also, as living stones, are being built up as a spiritual house for a holy priesthood, to offer up spiritual sacrifices acceptable to God through Jesus Christ. 1 PETER 2:5

Jamie came home from camp carrying a large rock with tiny rocks attached. He said, "Mommy, this is our rock family I made at camp."

"Tell me all about it."

"Jesus is our rock, so that's the big rock. I have stones for each of us. The tall skinny one is Dad. The pretty one next to it is not as tall, and that's you." He pointed to a more colorful stone.

Jamie pointed out four pebbles that represented his sisters, brother, and himself, with the littlest sparkly one as his little sister. All the little people had wiggle eyes glued on, and the stones were glued on the top of the big rock. Jamie chose each because he saw something in the stone that reminded him of the person.

Mom said, "We can put this in the garden by the front door." Jamie carried it out and found a spot right beside the bottom step to the house. They read about God as *Yahweh Tsuri*, the immovable rock of salvation in Deuteronomy 32:4 and 1 Samuel 2:2 and also read about people called living stones as part of God's family in 1 Peter 2:4-5.

Boys love rocks and stones. They see them as nature's building blocks and important treasures to collect and save. They like the strength and hardness of rocks. God likes rocks too. He made them, scattered them around the world, and carved them into mountains. Stones and a big family rock made a good welcome for visitors.

Hoelun's Remarkable Son, Genghis Kahn (Historic Mom)

I can do all things through Him who strengthens me.
PHILIPPIANS 4:13

As a widow, deserted by her clan, Hoelun hunted for berries and roots to feed her extended family. They lived in Mongolia, a rugged and barbaric country, in the twelfth century. She had four sons and a daughter but also took care of her children's half-brothers and their mother. Her sons fished with hooks they made from needles. They lived in poverty, but she cared for her children as best she could. She scolded them when they argued and said, "Why not agree and gain strength against enemies?" She grieved when two of her young sons killed a half-brother.

Hoelun cherished family. As a single mom, she overcame obstacles and struggled to help her family survive harsh winters and the wild country. Her love was stronger than her fears.

One of her sons grew to be the famous conqueror, Genghis Kahn. Hoelun became one of his most trusted advisors. Although a harsh warrior, he allowed freedom of religion.

Hoelun heard that Genghis planned to kill one of his brothers and raced over to his camp. She stepped out of her cart, untied her son Kassar, and yelled at Genghis. She pulled open her top and said, "See these breasts of mine, both of you? Ye two have drunk from them." She wanted them to realize her love and her nurturing united them.

Genghis replied, "I was frightened when I acted. I am ashamed at the moment." Sparing the life of her son was the greatest gift Genghis gave his mother. Hoelun never gave up on keeping her family united in love. One great desire of mothers is to see their children live in harmony and be friends for life.

Quarters for a House

A poor widow came and put in two small copper coins, which amount to a cent. MARK 12:42

Darlene held up four quarters and said, "Mommy, I want to give you all the money I saved. Use it for our new house so we can be with daddy."

Darlene's daddy had to work several states away while they waited for their home to sell and bought a new one. She missed her daddy and wanted her family to be together again. Mommy hugged Darlene tightly and said, "Thank you. This will be your house too, and you have a big part in it with helping us with your coins. Let's pray God will help us move soon."

Darlene prayed, "God, please help us be with my daddy. We miss him and we need you to help us be able to move soon."

Giving all her coins was a big sacrifice, but it made her mother feel better since she wanted the family together too. Little ones don't understand money and its value, but they are so willing to sacrifice. God can use little gifts from the heart, and those little gifts can also warm a mother's heart and bring hope when prayer answers seem to take so long.

Children also don't realize the sacrifices moms and dads make. Moms spend countless hours cleaning, cooking, and driving. The little gifts from children are their payment.

Darlene and her family waited months to be together

Today's Mom Step

Value your child's sacrifices and know that all you do, every little task of cleaning and more is a sacrifice for your family that God sees and values.

and moved without selling the house, borrowing money from family, but they rejoiced when they reunited in a little apartment as they built a house. And her coins added to the money they used to buy their home.

Week 6

Words Begin in Our Hearts

Prayer for a Heart Overflowing with Love

Gracious Lord, help me control my tongue and use it to encourage and not tear down. Let peace and love fill my heart so the words that come forth express love and joy. May I rejoice with my children's successes, empathize with their sorrows, and laugh with them over silly things. Let me heart overflow with love so that the words that I speak will be kind and loving.

Help me encourage the curiosity of my little ones, inspire my youngsters to enjoy learning and conversing, and engage my teens in adult discussions. Let us develop strong communication skills that keep us connected.

Help me listen with my heart to understand my children. Give me wisdom to respond to their needs with words that give them hope and answer their questions.

Help me share my faith in you so they will want to know and follow you.

Thanks for your words that I can echo every day to fill my heart with love.

Wisdom from Future Moms

Mom gives me two weeks of the same chores if mine are not done.

Mom, I'm okay if God doesn't help make be good today. I'm having a good time the way I am.

Hey, That's Not Fair!

Do all things without grumbling or disputing; so that you will prove yourselves to be blameless and innocent, children of God above reproach in the midst of a crooked and perverse generation, among whom you appear as lights in the world. PHILIPPIANS 2:14

"Mom, he got more ice cream than I did."

"Why did he get to choose a cookie first and take the biggest one?"

"Hey, why did she get to choose the show to watch?"

These are common words of children. Whining can escalate when it is not nipped in the bud. Terry decided she'd change things up for her family.

The next time a child complained that a sibling got more ice cream or a bigger slice of cake, she responded sweetly, "I would not want you to lie, and since I worked hard to share the food evenly, I will make sure your words are true." She scooped ice cream or part of the cake from the grumbler and put it on the sibling's plate. She added, "I work hard to make cookies and use the same size scoop for each one. I always hope you will be happy to get a treat." When one complained about a show, that child missed out on watching anything. That quickly stopped the comparisons and complaining.

Terry wanted grateful hearts, not ones seething with jealousy. They chatted as a family about grateful hearts and being thankful for whatever they receive. She asked. "Would it be better if I blindfold all of you before dessert, so you would not be tempted to compare portions?" They didn't want that. Then she offered treats

GROWING A MOTHER'S HEART

for anyone ready to praise God for the blessing of a snack. As they munched, each expressed thanks for a blessing.

Terry also made sure she praised God and her children aloud.

Divisive Words (Biblical Mom, Rebekah)

Now Isaac loved Esau, because he had a taste for game, but Rebekah loved Jacob. GENESIS 25:28

It's hard when parents favor one child over another. That favoritism begins in the heart and flows out in words and actions. Isaac, Abraham and Sarah's son, married Rebekah. They had twin boys, Esau and Jacob. Each parent chose a favorite rather than simply loving both sons equally. You can read the real problem that caused in Genesis 27. Basically, near the end of Isaac's life, Rebekah encouraged Jacob to disguise himself as Isaac to steal his brother's blessing. She even said that any curse for the deceit should be put on her.

Blessings from father to child were super important in those days, even bigger than inheriting wealth. Isaac blessed Jacob and asked God to give him an abundance of grain, leadership over people and his brother, and other blessings. Esau cried out with anger and held a grudge against Jacob when he discovered the scam. Rebekah sent Jacob away saying that Esau planned to kill him. They remained separated for fourteen years and both their parents died with a broken family. Rebekah, at the end of her life, said she was tired of living.

Rebekah had started out as such a lovely woman, eager to marry Isaac. When she was

> **Today's Mom Step**
>
> Bring your children together and complement each one for a unique attribute and pray for God to bless each one.

infertile, Isaac prayed for her, and God opened her womb, and she conceived these boys. She should have resolved to love both of them with all her heart. A mother's heart needs to love all and want the best for every child. Positive words will unite and not divide children. Praising the good actions of each child to their dads will show approval of all children and inspire dads to also accept and approve of each one.

Mother Echoes

Pleasant words are a honeycomb, sweet to the soul and healing to the bones. PROVERBS 16:24

Ever hear yourself saying something your mother said like, "Do as I tell you," "You're so clumsy." Or some other negative comment? You probably resolved not to be like your mother, yet here you are, repeating some of her negative phrases and causing the same hurt you felt as a child.

Abigail heard herself repeat such phrases. Even worse, her children echoed her negative tone and words with statements like,

"It's not fair."

"Why do I have to do this every day?" Or…

"Why does God bless that person and not me?" Abigail cringed! It seemed like their home was filled with negative words. She worked at being more positive in tone and words.

Soon, she smiled as she heard kind words from her children:

"Thank you so much!"

"You look so cool today mom. Your eyes even sparkle." Or…

"Thanks for the snack. You made my day."

Abigail found that starting the day reading or repeating an uplifting scripture filled her heart with positive thoughts. To focus positive attributes of her children she listed three good things about each child daily. That inspired her to speak kindly and be more forgiving of little mistakes. She used a smile and positive words to ask her children to do something, like, "Sweety, please put your beautiful clothes away, and then we can have a snack and chat. I like those jeans on the bottom of the pile. They seem to make

you look taller." Her children responded to sweet words and also started being more pleasant.

Speaking the Language, Elisabeth Elliot (Historic Mom)

Be strong and courageous, do not be afraid or tremble at them, for the Lord your God is the one who goes with you. He will not fail you or forsake you. DEUTERONOMY 31:6

Ten months after giving birth to her daughter, Valerie, natives in Ecuador called Aucas by other tribes (meaning savages), killed her husband and four other missionaries. Elisabeth and another of the widowed missionary women, continued the work. A woman who had fled the tribe helped them learn the language. They introduced her to other tribal women. A few years later, with her three-year-old daughter strapped to her back, Elisabeth trusted God and moved in with the tribe. She lived with the Aucas for a few years and returned to the states when Valerie turned eight.

Elisabeth always encouraged her daughter. Her example planted a deep faith in Valerie who later served with her husband as a missionary in Africa. She lived with the people who killed her father and watched her mother forgive them. Elisabeth showed her daughter how to see life from a positive perspective. Valerie viewed life in the jungle as an exciting playground and saw creation as gifts from God.

As a mother of eight, Valerie chose to mother like her mother did. She suggests if a child refuses to eat a certain food, to simply say nothing. Wait a few months, try that food again. It's better than saying, "You don't like that food," since those words reinforce that thought and lodges in their brains. No comment lets the children remain open to trying it later. Applying this same approach to other activities keeps a child's mind open to courage and prepares them to try again after failures.

Today's Mom Step

Encourage your child's sense of adventure and courage with a positive perspective and encouraging words.

Sprinkles of Joy While Shopping

Let your speech always be with grace, as though seasoned with salt, so that you will know how you should respond to each person. COLOSSIANS 4:6

As a child, Lisa loved shopping with her mother. She listened and watched as her mom always said something encouraging to the workers. She'd compliment someone's eyes, smile, or jewelry. Or she thanked the person for their help or hard work. It's no wonder that Lisa became a shopper when she grew up. Today, she shops for groceries and delivers them. She loves shopping and seeing the workers smile.

The workers are always happy to help Lisa and greet her when they see her. They know her name, and she knows their names. Now when her children go with her to buy their groceries or to shop for shoes, they also greet the workers and compliment them. The workers wave when they spot the children.

At Christmas, Lisa and her children make plates of cookies and deliver them to the stores for the workers. They make chocolate chip cookies, peanut butter balls, sugar cookies, and coconut macaroons. The cashiers and clerks respond with hugs and thanks. Later in the week as Lisa shopped, she received compliments and more thanks for such great treats. A few add, "You made my week!"

It only takes seconds to smile and pay a compliment, but it remains with the person much longer as they replay the words in their minds. It begins relationships and models graciousness that children catch.

> **Today's Mom Step**
> As you go out with your children be gracious, so they will hear you speak words of encouragement to the people you encounter.

Week 7

Gifts of Failure

Prayer to Learn from Failure

Lord, thank you for letting us fail. I cannot prevent my toddler from falling down, but I can applaud when my little one gets back up and takes another step. Lord, please help me let my children fail so they will become overcomers. I will be there to love my child in the face of failures and trust you will use it to strengthen both of us.

Give me courage to let my child fail. I will rejoice when my child tries again and succeeds.

You watched your only Son Jesus die on a cross. You knew that would bring the greatest victory of life for all believers. You will be with me in the face of all the ups and downs of motherhood. That promise will help me wait and trust that you know what's best for my precious children.

Wisdom from Future Moms

When I cry, mom lets me sit on her lap and cuddle with her. Then I feel better.

Mom gives us chores to learn to keep a house clean. It's sad for mom. Most of the time we fail on cleaning up.

Restart the Day

Behold, I will do something new, Now it will spring forth; Will you not be aware of it? I will even make a roadway in the wilderness, Rivers in the desert. ISAIAH 43:19

Eddy said, "Mommy you sound grumpy. Do you need to go back to bed like I do sometimes?"

Lisa smiled and said, "Maybe I do. I am sorry I yelled at you and got upset when you spilled milk and I slipped in it. You eat your cereal and I'll be back in a little while. I'm taking my Bible with me."

Back in bed Lisa read and prayed. She smiled as she thought of days Eddy woke up grumpy and everything seemed to go wrong before she suggested they start the day over. She needed a fresh start. She should have gently reminded him to keep the bowl away from the table's edge. She could have been kinder when it spilled, and she watched tears rolled down his cheeks. Even mom's need to adjust their attitudes. Lisa got up again and even changed clothes for a fresh start.

Waltzing into the kitchen, Linda hugged Eddy and said, "Forgive me for yelling. Let's take a walk and look for bugs." Eddy ran to grab his butterfly net, baseball cap, and put on his shoes. He held his mother's hand.

Eddy laughed, "I love finding bugs. I forgive you. Can you take pictures?"

Today's Mom Step

Be ready to forgive, apologize, and make a fresh start as needed.

"Sure. I've got my phone."

"Mommy, starting the day over really helps you too."

"Yes, we all need second chances and fresh starts. Forgiveness is so great. I'm glad God gave us that gift."

They went off on their bug hunt.

Midwives Fail to Obey (Biblical Moms, Shiphrah and Puah)

But the midwives feared God, and did not do as the king of Egypt had commanded them, but let the boys live. EXODUS 1:17

Shiphrah and Puah disobeyed Pharaoh's order to kill Israelites babies as the women gave birth. Pharaoh could have killed them for that and yelled at them, "Why have you done this thing and let the boys live?"

Pharaoh saw the Israelites' population increase and feared that they might rise up and rebel against their enslavement to the Egyptians. The women replied, "The Hebrew women are vigorous and give birth before we arrive."

God spared these two women and turned things around for them. He gave them families of their own. Failure to obey a law of humans was not failure to God. Choosing life brought them joy. Pharaoh then had his people toss any Israelite baby boys into the Nile River to die. Pharaoh did not value the lives of these babies.

God remained in control. He sent Moses with plagues to show His power and freed His people and brought them to safety. It's no wonder that God turned the Nile to blood, as this plague depicts loss of life. The last plague God sent to force Pharaoh to free the Israelites was the angel of death to kill the firstborn sons of the Egyptians, and thus Pharaoh lost his first son. The man who wanted to kill sons lost his own son. God let Pharaoh's own judgment return onto him.

> **Today's Mom Step**
>
> Whatever you fear, whatever seems to have a hold on you, give it to God and let Him help you turn failure to victory and fear to courage.

Moses freed God's people. The Israelites never had to lift a fist as God sent Moses and plagues.

God can turn things around. Trust that God knows best and be willing to adapt.

Who Are You to Take Away Her Dreams?

Do not merely look out for your own personal interests, but also for the interests of others. PHILIPPIANS 2:4

Nora and Frank met with the principal. Nora said, "My daughter Marie came home from school sobbing because you told her she had to take the vocational track. She wants to be a nurse."

"Well, we feel she is having a hard time with math and would need to repeat the grade."

Frank replied, "Who are you to take away her dreams? What will it matter if she repeats math, and takes an extra year to reach her goal and enjoy her future? She's willing to work as hard as needed."

"She could become an aid."

Nora said, "She has bandaged everyone including the dogs and the cow since childhood. She walked to the library to take the Red Cross First Aid class, the only teen in the class. It's all she's ever wanted. Her aunt teaches high school math and will tutor her."

"Let me talk with her teacher."

"We want to talk with the teacher with you. We'll wait."

The teacher listened and agreed that Marie could try and if needed, repeat the class and grade if it meant that much. Marie did repeat math. She worked hard and passed the class the next year. She became a nurse although she had to have help with math and study hard. Her patients loved her because she was so encouraging and patient.

When Frank had a heart attack and needed special nursing, Marie gladly helped cared for her father with the skills she learned. She felt grateful to help her parents who supported her dream.

Today's Mom Step

Listen to your child's dreams and consider how to support them.

Turning Loss into a Gift to the World (Historic Mom)

I have prayed for you, that your faith may not fail; and you, when once you have turned again, strengthen your brothers. LUKE 22:32

Harriet Beecher Stowe faced a tragedy no mother wants to face. Her second son Samuel Charles died of cholera at eighteen months old. She grieved the loss of this child, but it also made her understand the sorrow of slaves who had their families torn apart and children taken from them. The failure to save her son's life inspired Harriet to write her famous book *Uncle Tom's Cabin* and led her to be a strong abolitionist.

Harriet also survived other tragedies. Her son, Henry Ellis, drowned during his college years. Another son, Fredrick, struggled with alcoholism for many years, leading Harriet to write about alcoholism as a disease. She stuck by her son's side and encouraged her daughters to understand that his struggle against sin was no weaker than other struggles with sins but had more fatal and dreadful consequences. Just as she used her book to help people understand the plight of slaves, she used words to help her children accept the weaknesses of their siblings.

She visited Frederick when he served in the Civil War and nursed him after his injury in the Battle of Gettysburg. He traveled to California to go to sea in hopes of curing his addiction but later disappeared, and she never heard from him again. She grieved daily for the loss.

Harriet continued on with her family and her writing. Her

unmarried twin daughters assisted her, especially with correspondence. Her children served as the inspiration for characters in books she wrote, and her mother's love shines through the pages.

Am I a Teaching Failure?

And He said to them, "Cast the net on the right-hand side of the boat and you will find a catch." So they cast, and then they were not able to haul it in because of the great number of fish. JOHN 21:6

Darlene struggled again with her daughter's reading assignments. Elizabeth cried and said, "You taught Joseph to read, but I'm too stupid. I can't read. "

Darlene said, "You learn differently, and I need help to know how to help you."

That evening Darlene talked with her sister. "Rebecca you're a teacher. What can I do? Elizabeth is not getting it. She knows her letters and sounds, but she should be on a third-grade reading level, and she's not."

Rebecca said, "Let's have her visit me for a week. I'll test her and work with her."

Elizabeth spent a week with her aunt. She loved her time and worked hard. When Rebecca drove her home, she suggested a reading plan to Darlene. Elizabeth needed more encouragement but was progressing fine. Each day, she would read an easy book to her younger sister Julia to affirm her ability. Then she needed to read a higher level one to build confidence, and then a few pages from an even higher level to further increase her ability. Elizabeth kept improving.

Julia enjoyed listening to Elizabeth read. Elizabeth also helped them learn to read. Darlene smiled and praised Elizabeth saying, "I'm happy my sister helped us. We both needed to find what worked."

Elizabeth said, "I really can learn and I'm reading better. I love Aunt Rebecca." Elizabeth became an excellent reader, and Darlene learned to try something different when any of her children had a hard time with a subject.

> **Today's Mom Step**
>
> Identify something hard for you to do. Ask a friend and seek a new method or technique to try.

Week 8

The Mama Bear in Us

Prayer for Motherly Courage

Dear Lord, I want to protect my children and keep them safe. You understand my desire for you, and you declared you wished you could gather the Israelite children together as a mother hen gathers her chicks under her wings (Matthew 23:37). Let me not be a helicopter mom who smothers her children. Let me not be careless or distracted when I should protect them so they will feel secure. Help me assure them of both my love and trust in them.

Let me trust you to keep them safe, for your love for each child is unlimited. Help me guide them rather than dictate, train them with love, and let go as needed. Free me from worrying constantly and help me remain calm when they fall. Let me wait for them to persist and get up rather than rush to pick them up.

I want my children to be confident and strong and not depend on me for every step they take. Give me courage to be a mother bear only when really needed and to be a patient mom who lets her child learn to stand strong. When needed, give me the courage to speak up and defend my children.

Wisdom from Future Moms

What my mom does best is get my sister to stop hitting me.

I think my brother wants to be a mom, but it won't work. He tries to make all the rules when we play.

Cut Down to Size

This you know, my beloved brethren. But everyone must be quick to hear, slow to speak and slow to anger. JAMES 1:19

Debbie Wilson marched over to her neighbors, with her son and his visiting friend in tow. When her neighbor answered the bell smiling, Debbie said, "Can we talk?"

Heart pounding, Debbie tried to keep her voice level as she explained how her neighbor's son and her own son's visiting friend had misused her son and his friend. Her son had ended up covered in mud and grass stains from being pushed down-hill. The neighbor's eyes widened. "I saw the whole thing. Let me share what I saw." She called her son to see if he could add anything.

"I watched them roll down the hill on the grass and run back up to do it again. They also took turns starting the other one roll-ing. They pushed, then giggled and laughed. On your son's last turn down he picked up speed and landed in the mud. He stood up and yelled, "My mom's gonna be so mad at me for getting dirty." He raced home, and his guest trailed behind him. I see he changed his clothes."

Debbie turned to her son expecting him to step up with something they'd omitted. Instead he and his friend averted her eyes and tried to slink away. Their reluctance to face those they'd accused said it all. Debbie sighed, embarrassed for falsely accusing the boys. She'd let her son's emotions overwhelm her reason and send her off without all the facts. She apologized and thanked her neighbor for clearing up

> **Today's Mom Step**
>
> Check the facts when your child tells a tale of gloom.

the confusion. Then she turned to her son, and said, "It's time for your visiting friend to go home. We need to talk." She explained that honesty is much more important than dirt.

Precious Time (Biblical Mom, Jochebed)

The woman conceived and bore a son; and when she saw that he was beautiful, she hid him for three months. EXODUS 2:2

Pharaoh wanted him dead, but Jochebed could not let her beautiful son go easily. She wanted him to live and hid her son for three months, as long as possible. She covered a wicker basket with tar and pitch to make it waterproof, gently placed her son inside the basket, and then set it in the Nile River, near the bank among the reeds. As it floated away, she asked her daughter Miriam to keep watch.

Miriam watched as Pharaoh's daughter spotted the basket. She looked at the baby and felt pity. Miriam bravely walked up and asked, "Shall I go and call a nurse for you from the Hebrew women?" Pharaoh's daughter agreed and offered to pay the nurse. Miriam reunited her mother as the nurse for Moses. Jochebed had a few years with her son until she he stopped nursing. Then she brought him to Pharaoh's daughter, who named him Moses because she drew him out of the water. The joy of more time with a son and yet the grief of giving him up a second time must have been so difficult. She experienced a roller coaster of emotions: fear, joy, grief, and hope.

Not much else is known about this Jochebed. Her daughter helped her, and they must have shared a strong bond. Miriam led the people in a dance of joy once Moses brought them across the Red Sea. We know Aaron, Moses's older brother, became the assistant to Moses when God called Moses to free His people.

The closeness of family remained in spite of the hardship of separation.

Today's Mom Step

Nurture time together and praise children when they are kind to a sibling and help one another.

Jochebed used the time she had with her family to build lasting bonds. Most moms have 18 years. As a Mother Jochebed choose to keep her son Moses safe and made the most of every opportunity.

Whipped Up Trouble

Learn to do good; Seek justice, Reprove the ruthless, Defend the orphan, Plead for the widow. ISAIAH 1:17

Marie answered the phone to discover the principal had suspended her eight-year-old son Sean from school. Unraveling the story took a while. Sean, the last person on a game of whip at recess, let go of the girl's hand beside him. She fell on the pavement and hurt her head. One teacher rushed to help the girl and another marched Sean to the principal's office. The call brought out the momma bear in Marie.

Marie asked, "Why did teachers let children play whip?"

The principal had no answer to that or the other questions like, "Don't you know children whip around and expect some will lose the grasp of hands and fall down?"

"Why did they play on a hard surface and not even the grassy area?"

"How many children played and got suspended, including the first one who determined the whip's speed?"

"What has been done to discipline the teachers who neglected to keep the children safe? It is their responsibility not that of a child."

He had no answers to her questions.

Marie also chatted with the girl's mom since they were good friends. The mother was upset because she too thought the teachers caused the problem, so she also complained to the principal. She defended Sean who could only hold on for so long.

Marie appealed to the school board about the suspension. The principal called to apologize the next day and stated they reversed the suspension. Sean would be given

A's for any work missed since he generally earned A's. He also disclosed that the teachers had been instructed to stop any dangerous games under their playground supervision.

Captive Sons (Historic Mom)

The Spirit of the Lord GOD is upon me, because the LORD has anointed me to bring good news to the afflicted; He has sent me to bind up the brokenhearted, to proclaim liberty to captives and freedom to prisoners. ISAIAH 61:1

Roseanne Farrow, in the summer of 1780, received word that the British had captured three of her sons. She also learned she could trade British prisoners in exchange for colonial prisoners but needed two British prisoners for each colonial captive. She rode off to the colonial army camp where she explained the problem and asked for six prisoners. Colonel William gave her six captives plus a guard.

Roseann rode into the enemy camp with the captives to see the British preparing to hang her sons. They stopped. She bargained for the trade. She stated that she made her best trade ever, as her sons would whip their men four to one.

One of her captured sons, Samuel Farrow, became a lawyer and statesman who supported his new country and served others with a passion. He helped raise funds to build a school for the deaf and dumb and an asylum for the mentally ill.

A mother bear in the wild, especially a big brown grizzly, shows its fierce protective instincts and selflessly puts itself between her cub and the danger. The cubs watch the mother hunt for food and catch fish. That's how they learn.

Today's Mom Step

When you lock a door, buckle a car seat, and do other little safety steps, smile and know your children are watching and that your care gives them assurance.

A mother's example of sacrifice and hard work influences her children and shows them how much she cares. It demonstrates compassion and shows them she cares about their future.

The Last Straw

You will know the truth, and the truth will make you free. JOHN 8:32

When Peter arrived home from kindergarten, his mom, Telly, took one look at his face and knew something happened. He explained that he got in trouble for throwing Karl's straw on the floor.

That puzzled Telly, and she asked, "Doesn't he sit on the opposite side of the room?" Peter nodded. Did you get out of your seat?"

Peter shook his head and explained, "No. Karl came over holding his milk. He teased me until I pulled his straw out of the drink and threw it. I did not touch Karl."

Telly thought, "This is the last straw for me." When the teacher called and said Peter had been aggressive toward Karl, Telly asked, "Why was Karl across the room out of his seat?"

"I'm not talking about Karl."

"Did you notice that Peter remained in his chair and never touched Karl?"

"This is about your son."

"It took two children to have an incident. You brought up Karl. My son did not go near Karl's seat, and he did not touch him. Karl again bullied and teased my son."

The next day, Telly showed up with Peter. She handed the teacher index cards, stamps, and an ink pad. She asked, "Will you please stamp a card each time you see Peter doing something correct like sitting in his seat, handing in his work, and talking nicely with other children? I want you to notice when he is good." The teacher agreed. Soon she strung a clothesline in the room and hung up cards

> **Today's Mom Step**
> Use questions to make someone accusing your child think about what really happened.

for all the children to reward good behavior. That also helped the new teacher realize how much Karl caused problems for various children.

Week 9

You Are Significant!

Prayer for Significance

Lord, somedays I feel so unseen except by my children. In the midst of laundry piles and endless dishes and dust, I wonder if what I do matters beyond the walls of my home. Then you remind me I am valuable, and I am loved. Every mother is significant as we raise tomorrow's leaders and parents. At birth, we are the most important person in our child's life and one of their greatest influences throughout life.

Let my love for my children and You shine as an example for other moms. Let my actions instill character in my children. I'm grateful that your promises include blessing my family.

Guide me to where I can serve others with the little time I have. Help me impact the people I meet even if it is simply smiling and giving an encouraging word. Like the woman who gave a few pennies, may the minutes and hours I give to serve make a difference. Like the little boy who gave his sack lunch fed many people with your miracle, may you multiply my offerings and actions.

Help me today to use words of encouragement and smiles to bless my children and anyone we encounter.

Wisdom from Future Moms

I want to teach my child my children math, reading and science. And doing art projects and cooking meals. Then they will be great.

That's what I've been telling you, Mommy! When you grow up, you've got to BE somebody!

Chalk It Up!

Whatever you do, do your work heartily, as for the Lord rather than for men. COLOSSIANS 3:23

Darlene delivered groceries. This allowed her to earn money to pay bills while homeschooling when her husband went back to school. A trivial job, but she chose to be kind and loving. Darlene smiled and got to know her customers. She developed relationships with regular customers and worked hard to please each one, texting if a desired item was out of stock and letting them know alternative choices. She prayed for her customers. They cheered for her when she hit milestones like two thousand orders delivered. She gave customers a cupcake to celebrate her progress.

When the COVID-19 pandemic started, she continued working and observed safety. The manager let Darlene in early and set up a system for her to get paper goods and other hard-to-find items for her customers. They knew she also served people who stayed home due to high-risk health conditions. Her work doubled as people stayed home and sought her out to shop for them.

With the quarantine, Darlene missed seeing her customers and their families and the hugs they gave her. More work meant more pay but also added to the physical drain. Her back and ankles often hurt, but she kept going to help people who needed to stay home and to help her family.

Today's Mom Step

As you do your own chores with love today, pray for the people you serve.

One day as she drove to a customer's home, she noticed the gaily decorated sidewalk. Wow! Her customer's sweet daughter used chalk to say, "We love you Darlene" and added hearts, a rainbow, and bright colors to thank her. That made her day and helped her realize people cared about her and appreciated the work.

Every task, especially when done with love, makes a difference.

Rahab: From Sordid Past to Future of Hope (Biblical Mom)

In the same way, was not Rahab the harlot also justified by works when she received the messengers and sent them out by another way? JAMES 2:25

Harlot. That description remained forever linked with this woman in a good way. Her past became part of her testimony to bring hope. God used her and blessed her greatly.

Joshua became the leader of the Israelites after Moses died. He led the people into the promised land. Jericho remained a challenge. The Israelites failed to trust God and face this challenge under Moses. They listened to ten of twelve spies sent to check out the land and ended up wandering in the desert for forty years. Joshua only sent two spies, and they met Rahab. She welcomed them, and they stayed at her home. She saved them and stated that she knew about their God who parted the Red Sea and did mighty works. She asked the men to spare her and her family. They promised to be kind to her and asked her to tie a scarlet thread in her window so that they would remember where she lived when they returned to conquer the city.

The color scarlet is associated with sinful women. Yet that color ribbon saved Rahab and her family. The Israelites accepted her, and she married an Israelite.

Joshua followed the Lord's directions, and the great city of Jericho collapsed. German archeologists in 1907-09 discovered a portion of the northern wall had never collapsed. The construction indicated it was a poor section of the city and the likely location of Rahab's dwelling. After the fall of Jericho, Rahab and her family lived with the Israelites. She married Salmon and gave birth to Boaz, who married Ruth. Rahab and Salmon became the great-great-grandparents of King David. More than that, Rahab became an ancestress to Jesus Christ, the Hope of the world.

Today's Mom Step

Ask God to help you make the right choices today.
https://biblearchaeologyreport.com/2019/05/25/biblical-sites-three-discoveries-at-jericho/

Her choice to help two men made a difference to a nation.

One Stitch at a Time

So Peter arose and went with them. When he arrived, they brought him into the upper room; and all the widows stood beside him, weeping and showing all the tunics and garments that Dorcas used to make while she was with them. Acts 9:39

Kim cut fabric and started on another facemask to complete her 100th mask. Once finished, she scheduled a curbside pickup. She drove and dropped off the masks without needing to make contact. She also made a few surgical caps that someone requested and delivered them. She stayed home due to her high-risk health conditions and worked to help others stay away from the COVID-19 pandemic.

She heard about the need and looked up directions on how to make them. She had lots of 100-percent cotton fabric from her mother's handed down colorful quilt supply, and a man dropped off a few hanks of elastic. While her husband worked at home and her teens did their online classes, she cut and sewed. At a time when masks remained in short supply, each individual who sewed made a difference. Hundreds of people sewing added up to thousands of masks. Every stitch counted to keep people safe.

Kim chose favorite colors and designs to make masks for friends and family members. She cut the fabrics into the pieces needed and then started sewing. She stitched up a ninja-looking mask for her son, a ballet slipper print mask for her daughter, and a purple one for her mother-in-law. She gifted each loved one with something to make the person feel special and show she noticed what each one liked. Each person smiled and expressed thanks when they received their mask, giving her a distanced air hug.

> **Today's Mom Step**
>
> Keep track of people's interests and favorites (colors, foods, hobbies) and use the information when cooking or making something for the individual.

Mother Teresa and Helping One Person at a Time (Historic Mom)

Look at the birds of the air, that they do not sow, nor reap nor gather into barns, and yet your heavenly Father feeds them. Are you not worth much more than they? MATTHEW 6:26

Never actually a mother but a woman who loved whole-heartedly, Mother Teresa became known around the world for her faith and ministry. The plight of people in poverty touched her heart and she believed God called her to help. She left her traditional habit of a nun behind and donned a simple white cotton sari with a blue border. She studied basic medical training at Holy Family Hospital in Patna, India.

In 1949, Mother Teresa started a new religious community to help the poorest of the poor. She began by begging for food and necessities needed to help others. With little money and supplies, she simply started to help through small acts of kindness. As her ministry grew, she opened a hospice center for lepers, an orphanage, and other facilities in poor communities.

This remarkable woman, fluent in five languages, served as the mother of her organization. Father Joe listened to Mother Teresa on a regular basis during his years of studying for the priesthood in India. She impressed him with her care for others and her loving spirit. It's her nurturing spirit that caused so many people to respond. Today the organization has opened 700 homes in 136 countries and have sent their nuns to help after disasters.

Today's Mom Step

Rejoice that you are significant and take time to do small acts of kindness.

Mother Teresa did not look at a big plan, but like a good mother, looked at each individual who needed her. She became famous because she lived by her own motto, "Be faithful in small things, because it is in them that your strength lies." She focused on the person in front of her and one kind act at a time.

Cutting Paper

From whom the whole body, being fitted and held together by what every joint supplies, according to the proper working of each individual part, causes the growth of the body for the building up of itself in love. EPHESIANS 4:16

Carol called one of the moms in the Sunday school class she taught. She wanted to connect and also ask for help. Melissa answered, and they chatted. Melissa said, "I have a disabled son at home and can't get out to help."

Carol suggested, "Sometimes I really need someone to simply cut paper and prepare crafts for the children to make."

Melissa said, "I could do that. You can send the supplies home with my daughter."

That year, Carol sent home supplies about once a month, and Melissa faithfully followed instructions and prepared the materials. Her daughter would deliver them with a big smile and say that she also helped. Carol called every few weeks to express her appreciation and just to chat with Melissa. They became devoted friends. Carol also sent little gifts for Melissa and her family.

When the year ended, Melissa said, "I am so thankful I could help this year. My daughter loves helping me, and we both feel like we help the class. I don't feel so invisible."

"I can let the teacher she'll have next year know how you have helped."

"I'd like to continue helping you. I could do both classes. You make me feel like the little I do matters."

Today's Mom Step

Show appreciation by thanking people around you for the little acts of service they do.

Carol replied, "I am thrilled to have you help again. What you do matters to the children and me. In class we always thank God for your help. We all have our gifts, and you are much better at cutting than I am."

Week 10

Loving the Wildness

Prayer for an Adventurous Spirit

Dear Lord, I love the natural joy, wildness, and freedom I see in my child. The wildness also scares me as I fear my little one might get hurt, will never sit still, follow rules, or show good manners. Help me bring balance to my child without squelching that inner free spirit.

Help me let go and be wild at times too, with pillow fights, silly activities, and running in the yard or crossing a brook barefoot. Help me foster my child's curiosity and natural sense of adventure to explore and discover the world with the natural playgrounds you created.

Let me balance the need for order with my child's need for learning through play. Let me rejoice at the giddiness of finding a bug, seeing a monkey climb, and the fun of imitating what is seen. Help me balance discipline and training to develop focus and build skills like music, educational pursuits, and athletic ability.

Help me share my child's exuberance for life and inspire my child's God-given bent. Let their sense of adventure also develop courage. Help me be brave enough to seek adventure and trust you will keep me safe.

Wisdom from Future Moms

I wish mom could squirt my feet like she does the rug and furniture when they stink. She makes me take a bath.

Mommy teaches me to be polite. When my hiney burps I say, "Excuse me."

Boy-sterous

Therefore that disciple whom Jesus loved said to Peter, "It is the Lord." So when Simon Peter heard that it was the Lord, he put his outer garment on (for he was stripped for work), and threw himself into the sea. JOHN 21:7

The differences between Carrie's two children seemed like night and day. Her quiet book-loving daughter became such a great helper. Her noisy, boisterous son found reasons to laugh and race all day, overflowing with joy. He even dove off diving boards before he started walking and approached life with no fear.

On Christmas day, her daughter walked into the room filled with gifts, spotted a playhouse, smiled, and said, "That's just what I wanted." Her brother Shawn raced past her, ran into the playhouse, stuck his head out the window, and roared with laughter.

Her daughter turned and saw the firetruck she'd wanted and said, "The firetruck I asked for looks beautiful." Shawn jumped into the firetruck, rang the bell, and drove it.

The gentleness of her daughter helped her fit in school well as she sat and diligently did her work. Carrie encouraged her to join school groups and join in fun activities. Shawn seldom sat still, laughed in the classroom, and frustrated teachers. He always knew the right answers although he never seemed to pay attention. His teacher complained to Carrie all the time about his unruly behavior. Carrie wanted Shawn to be calmer, but she didn't want to take the bounce out of him. She enrolled him in soccer and swimming to channel the energy, gave him behavior pointers, and made sure he spoke politely.

At the end of the school year, she asked for a specific

Today's Mom Step

Embrace each child's uniqueness and find the best learning environment for each one.

GROWING A MOTHER'S HEART

teacher she knew allowed children more freedom when they finished their work. That worked. The room included a book nook with a loft where children who completed their work could climb up to read or use activity kits. She helped both her tamer and wilder children find their comfort zones.

Raising an Unruly Child (Biblical Mom, Samson's Mother)

Then Manoah entreated the LORD and said, "O LORD, please let the man of God whom You have sent come to us again that he may teach us what to do for the boy who is to be born." JUDGES 13:8

Manoah prayed for his wife to have a child and an angel appeared to his wife, saying, "you shall conceive and give birth to a son." The angel also explained the child would be a Nazarite. A Nazarite took a vow and dedicated himself to God. That meant the person agreed to abstain from any grape product, to remain clean and not go near a dead body, and never cut his or her hair.

They trusted God's promise but prayed for advice on raising the child. They received the response of raising the child as a Nazarite. Sometimes a child seems so smart or special, or has unusual needs, that it's hard to know what to do. Samson's parents' fear allowed them to let their son, Samson, control them instead of being parents who taught their child to make wise choices.

Samson told his parents, "I saw a woman in Timnah, one of the daughters of the Philistines; now therefore, get her for me as a wife." They lost the argument to their strong-willed child to find a more suitable woman, and ultimately helped him marry her. When a lion roared and attacked Samson, he killed it. He later found honey and bees in the carcass, ate it, and gave some to his parents. He broke the Nazarite vow and kept the incident secret. His lack of discipline and control caused problems.

He made other rash choices, lost his wife, but served as a judge and deliverer for Israel twenty years. Samson gave in to beautiful Delilah's selfish pleas and revealed the secret of his strength. That allowed his enemies to overpower him, cut his hair. He lost his strength, eyesight, and became a prisoner. At last, Samson cried out for God's help. God answered, and he defeated his enemies.

His parents had instilled faith in Samson, the one counter to all the wildness, the best parental choice made.

Climbing Trees

For you will go out with joy and be led forth with peace; the mountains and the hills will break forth into shouts of joy before you, and all the trees of the field will clap their hands. ISAIAH 55:12

Zach said, "Can you buy a house with a tree to climb? I know there won't be a cannon in the backyard like we have here."

The family sat around the table, as mom and dad asked what they each hoped for in a new home. With Dad's new military orders, they would not live on base. They would buy a house.

They wrote out the wish list of a room of my own, a big yard, and room for friends to come over. They drove a few hours and left the children with Sheila's parents and started house hunting. It took some time, but they chose a house that met the children's desires, including trees and even some big boulders to climb.

Many days, Sheila watched the children hanging off limbs and playing in the silver maple tree in the front yard or running and hiding among trees in the woods at the edge of the backyard. The breeze rustled the leaves and seemed to applaud the children. They also picked wild berries in the woods, raked colorful leaves in the fall, and jumped into the piles they made.

Zach often said, "I like our house and all the trees mom. You and dad made a good choice. I like the big rocks too. My friends think we have the best trees and rocks to climb. And the small rocks are fun to roll over to find bugs. We have lots of black beetles."

Sheila sat in her lawn chair and said, "I grew up with rocks and trees too. It's the best playground especially for

> **Today's Mom Step**
>
> Be sure to let your children roam outside to explore God's creation.

kids who like to run and explore. I'm glad you enjoy the great outdoors God made."

A Faithful Mother (Historic Mom, Monica, Mother of St Augustine)

Therefore, confess your sins to one another, and pray for one another so that you may be healed. The effective prayer of a righteous man can accomplish much. JAMES 5:16

In the fourth century, AD, Monica's heart broke, as she saw her son follow his wild streak and make poor choices. Her husband's violent temper added to her son's rebellious nature. As a youth, Augustine lived a life of a thief and playboy.

Monica, known for bringing peace to people at odds, prayed faithfully for her son. From the time he began his wayward life at age 16, she prayed continually. He used his brilliant mind in pursuit of truth and dug into different philosophies that disappointed him. Finally, in his early 30s, he turned back to the God of Christianity. His pride, lust, and doubts about faith kept him from following Jesus until he cried out to God in a garden in AD 386.

In response, he heard a voice like a child chanting, "Take and read! Take and read!" He opened his copies of Paul's letters to Romans 13:13–14, and the words changed him. The words spoke of putting on Christ and not the flesh, strife, or lust. Augustine describes the moment as one where light of relief from anxiety flooded into his heart and dispelled all doubt. He gave up all his sinful habits and his mother rejoiced that God answered her prayers.

Augustine wrote a detailed confessional account of his past and then started writing theological books. He became one of the early church fathers, and his writings are still studied. Monica rejoiced at her son's change and ministered in Africa with her son. She died a year after her son's conversion. His writings include references to the importance of his mother's prayers. In his confessions he shares his gratitude, "now gone from my sight, who for years had wept over me, that I might live in your [God's] sight."

> **Today's Mom Step**
> Make praying for each of your children a daily habit.

Noisy Neighborhood

And the streets of the city will be filled with boys and girls playing in its streets. Zechariah 8:5

Missy listened to the sounds of children's voices, basketballs bouncing and hitting the backboard, and children jumping rope. She heard the yells of jubilation as someone scored a basket and the ditties sung to the rhythm of jumping. She smiled as she worked with the happy sounds in the background.

Later that day, Missy chatted with her next-door neighbor, an empty nester, like herself. Her neighbor Terry said, "I can't stand all the noise the children make. The children are so wild and allowed to roam outside and play all day. How can you work at home?"

"Those are happy sounds to me. I miss the days when my five children played and made such similar noises. The children, from so many families, get along so well. Play helps them learn to socialize and cooperate. I'm thankful it's a safe place for them to play."

Terry said, "Once I retire, we're moving away and will not live in a community with so many children. You must be happy to have your house up for sale."

"I'm moving to be closer to family and some of my many grandchildren. I hope to find another community with lots of children. They give life to the neighborhood. The wildness is a freedom of spirit I appreciate. I enjoy having many of them over to make chocolates with me before holidays. They just speak freely and share what's on their minds. It's so refreshing."

"The moms all stop and chat with you. Was your home the gathering place?"

Missy replied, "Yes, and full of fun. You had the one child, and she is a quiet lady.

> **Today's Mom Step**
> Let children's noises be music to your ears.

Let the happy sounds be like music just as the sounds of birds flying and tweeting."

Week 11

How Can I Make the

Best Choices?

Prayer for Wisdom

Lord guide me in making wise choices for my family and myself. There are so many choices for the family: on finances, lifestyle, vacations, and more. There are choices with the children on how to train them, what activities to try, and how to nurture each one's individual talents. There's also the need to let my children make choices and understand the consequences.

Let me see the options and possible outcomes, and weight them carefully. Help me stop, think, and pray before I make a decision and not be impulsive.

Give me wisdom Lord and help me find the facts and understand the motives behind the choices. Give me wisdom and good mentors in my life. Help me have peace with decisions I make as a mom and not worry. Let me learn from my both my wise and foolish choices.

Help me to be a team player with making choices with my spouse. Help me listen to my children too, as they grow and want to discuss decisions. Help me trust them to make good choices and to encourage them to restart when they make poor choices. Help our family be content with choices made.

Wisdom from Future Moms

It's okay that mom works. That way she can buy things for me.

I don't think I wanna be a mama. I just wanna be a Gwamma when I gwow up.

The Diaper Bag

Discretion will protect you, and understanding will guard you.
PROVERBS 2:11

Rachel thought about her strong-willed daughter Penny. Even at three and a half years old, she wanted to be in control and take charge of everything. Rachel understood her daughter's personality and decided the best choice lay in giving Penny control over some little things. With a younger son and new baby, she'd love help with the diaper bag.

Rachel said, "Penny, I need your help. With your little brothers it's hard to get him ready and have everything ready or us to leave. So, would you take charge of the diaper bag? I need diapers and some other items to be in it at all times."

Penny grinned, "I know everything that goes in the bag. Diapers, wipes, a clean changing pad, rattles, snacks, and a blanket. I can do that mom. You won't have to worry about anything."

Yes, Penny took care of the diaper bag and didn't let anyone else touch it. She loved being in control of it and carried it to the car and back inside where she always checked the contents and replenished it. Penny wanted to do more and suggested she could choose the dinner vegetables and prepare them or make salad. She helped her mom choose the vegetables to buy and used an easy chopper her mother bought. She glowed at the praise for doing her jobs well.

As her brothers grew Rachel gave them appropriate jobs. Paul tended to forget to do things and didn't want to have so much control, but he enjoyed building his muscles with taking out the trash and recycles weekly. Jimmy, much quieter and younger, refilled the toilet

---

Today's Mom Step

Choose activities and task that fit your child's personality.

---

paper and napkins as needed. He liked being a quiet little checker and liked going around to see if he needed to refill anything.

Solomon's Wisdom for Two Biblical Moms
(Biblical Moms)

Then the woman whose child was the living one spoke to the king, for she was deeply stirred over her son and said, "Oh, my lord, give her the living child, and by no means kill him." But the other said, "He shall be neither mine nor yours; divide him!" 1 KINGS 3:26

Solomon, the wisest man who ever lived, made one of his toughest decisions ever when two women came to him with one baby boy. They lived in the same house and gave birth on the same night. One baby died. Each woman claimed she gave birth to the living infant and that the other woman's baby died in birth.

Solomon considered the situation and asked for a sword. He proposed dividing the baby in half. The real mother cried out and said to give the baby to the other women. She could not bear to see her son die. The woman whose baby had died agreed with the king and yelled to divide the child.

Solomon understood the heart of a mother. He wrote the famous lines of Proverbs 31 that describe a worthy woman. He knew the real mother would choose life for her baby. He proclaimed that the woman ready to sacrifice her role as mother to save her child revealed the truth and gave the child to that woman.

The other women cried out from anger and pain as a grieving mother who lost her child. She made a poor decision to steal her friend's baby

> **Today's Mom Step**
> For decisions you face today consider how it could impact your child's safety, growth, and future.

to fill the ache of her empty arms. Solomon did not punish the woman. He knew she already suffered.

What a great relief for the real mother. When we fear for our child's safety and then the child is safe, it brings great relief and renews our love. The bottom line in decisions for mothers is choosing what's safest and best for each child.

Work Choices

For which one of you, when he wants to build a tower, does not first sit down and calculate the cost to see if he has enough to complete it? LUKE 14:28

Dana juggled her schedule and figured out when she'd be home to play with her children and help with the home. She loved being with her baby, but she needed to work. Her husband stayed home to complete his schooling so he could get a good job. She already had a job that paid the bills.

At last Dana's husband graduated and got a job. Dana stayed home. She realized she had extra time as her first entered school, and she wanted to add to the income since it looked like the little ones needed private schooling. She loved photography and taking photos of her little ones. She started a family portrait business, especially portraits of new babies. She would schedule mostly to work weekends and times the children were in programs. She could also trade hours in her mom's babysitting coop.

Her business grew as the children grew. She made her own career that she ran from home. It took off, and she started to spend more time editing. She didn't want work to infringe on her time when the children were home. She decided to hire a video editor.

She found a mom with great experience and contract-

Today's Mom Step

As your children grow, choose how you will use manage the time, including your free time.

GROWING A MOTHER'S HEART

ed her. That freed up time and also allowed Dana to do more actual photography work. More clients offset the money she paid her worker. Yes, she could have a career and time with her children, but also make wise business choices regarding her time.

She still loved snapping photos of her children. As she captured various moments and posted about them, it also gave her ideas of photo packages clients might enjoy from their child's first time riding a bike to capturing memories of seasonal family fun.

Daring Choices (Historic Mom, Kernhappuch Turner)

Also this I came to see as wisdom under the sun, and it impressed me. ECCLESIASTES 9:13

Hearing of her son's (or grandson) injury in the Battle of Guilford Court House, Kerenhappuch Turner galloped on horseback as fast as possible the two hundred miles from Culpepper, Virginia, to Guilford, North Carolina. She rode through enemy lines and refused to accept the doctor's recommendation to amputate her son's leg.

Once she moved her son, James, to a bed in a log cabin near the battleground, this brave mother suspended a large tub of water over his head. She drilled holes in the tub and constantly poured cool spring water from Bloody Run river into the tub to let it drip onto the infected leg. Her choice to try something different relieved his fever and saved his leg. He served as a captain under General Greene in the American Revolution, although he walked with a limp.

The first monument erected to a woman from the American Revolution honored this mother. She also helped other wounded soldiers while ministering to her own son. They were sons of other mothers, and she had great compassion for those mothers and their sons. Once her son healed, this courageous woman served as a spy and courier. The British never suspected an old woman of serving the military.

The dedication of the monument honored mothers who sacrifice for their sons who serve It includes the words, "These ministers of compassion, these angels of pity, whenever possible, went to the battlefields to moisten the parched tongues, to bind the ghastly wounds, and to soothe the parting agonies alike of friend and foe, and to catch the last whispered messages of love from dying lips."

> **Today's Mom Step**
>
> Be courageous in making choices to help your children and the children of other mothers.

Pray and Plan

Commit your works to the Lord and your plans will be established.
PROVERBS 16:3

Cathy and her husband Bruce sat in the basement with their calendars opened up. The babysitter had their number to text if needed. This monthly meeting to pray over the family and make plans helped them guide their family and stay close as a couple.

Bruce said, "I think I've circled your busiest days on my calendar. I notice two fall on two of my busy days. Let's plan to order in or eat out then."

Cathy replied, "My day with all those doctor appointments is a good one to eat out as we can reward children for their checkups. The other one I'll have something in the freezer to pop in the oven. Let's look at each child."

One by one they reviewed the best news and most difficult problem of each child. They made plans to celebrate those bests

GROWING A MOTHER'S HEART

while encouraging the biggest struggles. They also thought of ways to use each child's talent or newly acquired skill that month. Timmy could read the scripture of the day to celebrate his reading progress, and Shelly could help wash and fold clothes to remember to care for her clothes and not drop them on the floor of every room. They planned an outdoor hike and a game night for two of the more open days and also scheduled a date night.

Bruce sat back and complimented Cathy, "I love how you calm the children when they start to argue. You've picked up some new techniques. I've copied them."

> **Today's Mom Step**
> Take time to pray, evaluate your children, and make family plans.

Cathy smiled, "Thanks! I read a great book. You always make the children and me laugh. I think about the comments all day to lift my spirits."

They ended the time with a prayer and prepared for the coming month.

Week 12

Letting Go

Prayer to Let Go and Trust God

Lord, every stage is a new opportunity for growth from the first step away from me and first time left with a sitter, learning to cook, and ride a bicycle, to eventually leaving home. Each new step will be a mix of joy and sadness. Help me rejoice as my child learns a new skill and takes a new step toward independence. Lessen my worries and help me let go at each stage.

Lord, give me the courage to let go of my precious child. My child grows faster than I ever imagined. I want the best for my child and know that means to equip this precious one to grow up and become independent. It's hard to hear each, "I can do it myself."

Help me to trust my child will make the right decisions and give me the wisdom to teach him how to make good choices. Help my child learn to be accountable to you.

Help me grow my mother's heart to be one that let's go and enjoys seeing my child soar and succeed.

Wisdom from Future Moms

When mom is sad, I just make silly faces, and that makes her laugh.

I wish mom would let go of some rules, like my bedtime. Then she wouldn't have to yell so much at night.

Do It Myself!

When I was a child, I used to speak like a child, think like a child, reason like a child; when I became a man, I did away with childish things. 1 CORINTHIANS 13:11

Two-year-old Joey ran out of the house and raced up the street. He seemed determined to escape. Finally, his mother decided to go with him. She followed him as he gleefully raced to the top of the hill and stopped at the mailbox. He wanted to climb it, so she picked him up. He opened the door and looked inside. Then she figured out his quest.

Joey's mom said, "Joey you just got a little mailbox that looks like this one. Yours is filled with blocks." He nodded and pointed at the big mailbox.

His mom said, "This mailbox does not hold blocks. It's to put in letters to send to people like your grandma. A mailman comes and takes them out to take them to the right people. Joey walked around the box and then started laughing. Like understanding a joke someone had played, he realized he was fooled. Back home he grabbed his little mailbox and played with the blocks. He stopped trying to escape, but still wanted independence in various ways every day.

> **Today's Mom Step**
> Applaud your child's new skills and capture memories with your camera and journaling.

Joey wrinkled his nose and shook his fists saying, "Do it myself!" His words echoed his older sister's toddler days. Whether getting dressed, pouring milk, choosing what to play with, including reaching for expensive knick-knacks, or walking without holding an adult hand, Joey's mom recognized and encouraged the safe choices. She reinforced needed rules

GROWING A MOTHER'S HEART

and rewarded him with extra playtime or new activities when he followed the rules.

She sighed and thought, "They want to grow up so fast, and I want him to grow, but part of me loves the little boy and wishes he'd stay that way longer. I must be willing to let go as he grows."

Letting Go So Soon (Biblical Mom, Hannah)

For this boy I [Hannah] *prayed, and the Lord has given me my petition which I asked of Him. So I have also dedicated him to the Lord; as long as he lives he is dedicated to the Lord." And he* [Elkanah] *worshiped the Lord there.* 1 SAMUEL 1:27-28

Clutching a little hand, still a child, Hannah gave her son into the care of the priest to serve in the temple. She had longed for a child, even prayed and wept for a son, yet vowed if God answered her prayer, she would give her son to God. She named him Samuel that means 'name of God' or 'God heard' because God did answer her prayer.

After giving birth to the son she desperately wanted, Hannah stayed home from the annual visit to the temple until she weaned him. Then she let go of her dear child. She and her husband Elkanah brought Samuel to the priest Eli. She visited Samuel once a year and brought him a new robe. Only one day a year did she see him, touch him, and talk with him. Eli, the priest, prayed for Hannah to have more children and God blessed her with three more sons and two daughters.

As soon as Hannah let go of her son, she and her husband praised God and rejoiced in the Lord. Then she returned home with her husband. She chose to be joyful and thankful she gave birth to a son. She trusted God. She didn't dwell on missing her son although she must have prayed for him as she wove the threads and sewed the robe that she'd give him the following year. She wove those prayers into each stitch.

When Samuel grew up, he became a judge, priest, and prophet for Israel. News of Samuel would have been spread widely once he took on those roles. How wonderful for his mother to hear of his great deeds.

> **Today's Mom Step**
> Trust God to help you relax and not be a helicopter mom.

Off to Camp

And who of you by being worried can add a single hour to his life?
MATTHEW 6:27

"Let's put each outfit in a plastic bag that zips close, to help it stay clean." Lucinda said and handed her daughter Layla a box.

They chatted while packing. Lucinda kept offering more suggestions until Layla said, "Mom, it's okay. Stop worrying because I'll be fine."

Lucinda said, "It's first time you're going away to a new place for a week."

Layla laughed and said, "Mom, that's only seven days. You'll survive. Enjoy yourself. I'm growing up. My best friend will be with me."

The next day, Layla's parents prayed with Layla and then dropped her off at a bus that would take her and many other kids to camp for the week. Lucinda's husband said, "Let's go to brunch, do some shopping, and catch a movie. You need to fill the day and not spend it missing our little girl."

The week dragged by for Lucinda, and she eagerly waited to see her daughter. She chatted with other moms whose daughters also went to camp. Those with older children helped her relax and trust that the kids would be fine.

Once home, Layla hugged her mom and said, "I had a great time. I want to go longer next year, like a few weeks."

Today's Mom Step
Give your child freedom in small steps.

Lucinda smiled and said, "I'm glad you enjoyed camp. You really are growing up."

"I have new friends and want to chat online with them. I also made a basket and necklace and learned to dive."

Doubting John (Historic Mom, Mary Machem)

You shall teach them diligently to your sons and shall talk of them when you sit in your house and when you walk by the way and when you lie down and when you rise up. DEUTERONOMY 6:7

John Gresham Machen (known as Gresham) began to doubt his faith when he met the liberal German theologian Herrmann while he studied in Germany, in 1905. His mother Minnie prayed about her son's struggles but chose to let go rather than lecture him. She wrote,

But one thing I can assure you of—that *nothing* that you could do could keep me from loving you—*nothing*. It is easily enough to grieve me. Perhaps I worry too much. But my love for my boy is absolutely indestructible. Rely on that whatever comes. And I have faith in you too and believe that the strength will come to you for your work whatever it may be, and that the way will be opened.

Minnie shared her faith with her three boys as she raised them. She read *Pilgrim's Progress* and the Bible to them and trained them in the *Westminster Catechism*. She homeschooled her sons. Gresham went on to John Hopkins University and then studied law and banking at the University of Chicago but changed direction and enrolled in seminary. The earnestness of Herrmann drew Gresham to consider his peculiar ideas that cast doubt on Christ's resurrection and other core beliefs.

His mother's unlimited love and her consistent faith drew Gresham back to follow the sound doctrine of his childhood. He served during the First World War, where he saw liberalism grow and chose to counter it. He established a new denomination, the Orthodox Presbyterian Church, and started writing, including his greatest work, *Christianity and Liberalism*. He considered his mother, the woman who let go, to be the wisest and best human he ever knew.[1]

> **Today's Mom Step**
>
> Trust God to help you relax and not be a helicopter mom.

When a Son Cleaves

For this reason a man shall leave his father and his mother, and be joined to his wife; and they shall become one flesh. GENESIS 2:24 (quoted in MATTHEW 19:5)

Neil introduced his girlfriend, Elly, to his mom. Marnie had met various girlfriends over the years but recognized little differences in her son. Her two older sons, already married, had shown the same signs. The protective arm, the longer glances, and the gentleness he showed for her all revealed a change. Her son was cleaving to this young woman, and they would become a couple.

Marnie recalled how one friend struggled when her son

---

1. https://www.challies.com/articles/the-unbreakable-bond-of-training-and-tenderness-christian-men-and-their-godly-moms/

became engaged to a woman she had enjoyed. The friendship turned into a struggle over her son and caused a rift that never fully healed. She realized her friend never let go, never wanted her son to leave the close relationship they'd had before his marriage. Marie had seen her other sons and her daughters marry. They needed to depend on one another and join together as one. Her role changed. It seemed easier with them because her husband was living when they married. Now, as a widow, she knew she needed to let go of her baby. His wife would become the center of his life and heart.

Marnie took time to get to know Elly, shared stories of her son as a boy, asked about Elly's early years, and enjoyed watching them grow closer. She'd ask them together when she wanted her son's help so they could decide the best timing and let them know whatever timing they chose would be fine. If her son drove them somewhere, she sat in the backseat even when Elly offered her the front seat. She noticed that made Elly smile. Afterall, she'd prayed for this woman for years, since Neil's childhood days. God also answered prayers for her son to grow and become a wonderful man. Letting go gave her a new daughter.

> **Today's Mom Step**
>
> Pray now for your children's future spouses and think of that person growing up too.

Week 13

Be My God-Created

Mom-Self

Prayer to Accept Myself

Dear Lord, in my quest and struggle to be the best mom I sometimes lose myself and try to be someone else. Help me be myself and accept the me you created. Let me build on my strengths and overcome my weaknesses. Let my children see the real me and appreciate what I do well. Help me laugh at my mistakes and let my family laugh with me.

Help me appreciate other moms and not compare myself to each of them. We are unique and can help one another the most when we accept and affirm one another. Let me grow a mother's heart that loves unconditionally and is not afraid to show my true colors nor afraid to work to improve myself.

Bring out the creativeness in me whether it's in the arts, social skills, organizing, or other area. Let me see the best in my children too and encourage them to be who you created them to be and not try to copy someone else. Let me model being my best self so my children will do the same.

Wisdom from Future Moms

When mom yells at me, I'm Pretty sure she does not mean it.

A mom took her daughter, age 3 or 4, into the store dressing room. The mom tried on dresses. Her daughter clearly disapproved of one that looked slightly frumpy and said, "That's a lady's dress! You're not a lady! You're a mommy."

Overall Mom

As each one has received a special gift, employ it in serving one another as good stewards of the manifold grace of God. 1 PETER 10:4

PeggySue Wells wore overalls everywhere. Her children teased her about her passion for buying the most outrageous overalls available. When everyone in her peer group wore dresses, their mama wore brightly colored, stylish overalls. Pink, blue, white, turquoise, and pinstriped. Long, short, and capri style. Even burgundy corduroy in winter. They reflected her personality. Her children still chat about her style and send photos when different designs come out.

Dressing in casual comfort helped PeggySue feel relaxed yet ready to face the day. White and blue, a favorite color combination, echoed her simplicity and loyalty. She listened well and helped other moms feel relaxed and less stressed when she felt comfy.

She gathered with other moms and they talked about fashion and their own styles. Organized Chrissy liked everything to be fitted and more tailored and always had answers to questions like how to get stains out and what food provided the needed nutrients. She avoided jeans, and that fit her reserved personality. Liz liked bold colors and suits where she looked like a director; that reflected her take-charge personality. Liz could handle all the kids easily and knew all about the best curricula to use. Zena wore bright prints and the latest fashion. She loved to make an entrance and be the life of the party, and it showed in what she wore. Zena made any gathering an event.

> **Today's Mom Step**
>
> Choose to be yourself and rejoice with others who express their unique personality too.

PeggySue enjoyed friends who chose to be themselves. She loved the different perspectives of each mom and how collectively they could rise to any challenge.

Unique Woman Judge (Biblical Mom, Deborah)

She [Deborah] *used to sit under the palm tree of Deborah between Ramah and Bethel in the hill country of Ephraim; and the sons of Israel came up to her for judgment. JUDGES 4:5*

No fancy desk and high-backed chair for this judge. Deborah, the wife of Lappidoth, chose to sit under a palm tree as she made decisions. She chose to work outdoors in the shade. God also gave Deborah the gift of prophecy. This woman chose to be herself as she confidently followed God's guidance and served as one of Israel's judges.

Deborah sent for Barak to lead the army into battle against the enemy led by Sisera. She said God had given the leader and his army into their hands to assure them of victory. Barak agreed to go if she would accompany him. His fear showed. She agreed to go, stated the honor or the victory would not be his. As a believer with great faith in God, his response fell short. She prophesied the honor would belong to a woman. Another wife, Jael, killed the enemy's leader.

The song of Deborah and Barak celebrated a great victory over the Canaanites, and her words included the phrase, "I, Deborah arose as a mother in Israel." The words praise God. Her motherly instinct shows up as with her words, "My heart goes out to the commanders of Israel, the volunteers among the people." That's not usually a phrase that men say to commanders before a battle.

The victory also brought peace to Israel for the forty years Deborah ruled. She served as one of the most outstanding and wise judges of Israel. Her name means "bee" or "a maker of honey." She brought her sweetness and peace to the people around her and had the courage to sting the enemy.

Running in Circles

I will give thanks to You, for I am fearfully and wonderfully made; Wonderful are Your works, and my soul knows it very well. PSALM 139:14

Cindy plopped herself down on a barstool by the kitchen counter and announced, "I'm beat after school and swim team, I need a break."

She watched her mom chase her little brother, Chris, around the wall that separated the kitchen from the hall. Her mother would switch directions and surprise her brother who giggled, turned, and raced away. They kept it up for several minutes before her mom grabbed Chris and carried him to a barstool and plopped him down.

Cindy said, "Mom I know why you have so many children. You never grew up and always like to play. But don't worry, since some of us are already teens, you'll have grandkids before Chris grows up. You don't need to have more."

Mom laughed and said, "I do love my five kids right down to the littlest one. I took a little break before the family started to arrive, so I'm reenergized." She said she'd fix a snack.

She smiled as she listened to the two chat about what they did that day. Chris asked Cindy to read a book, and she agreed, if he'd choose a short one. As she finished reading, mom placed a fun snack in front of them: banana slices, a dish of milk, and assorted toppings in separate bowls that included crushed nuts, coconut, and crushed cereal. They all started dipping a slice in the milk and then into a topping. Cindy said, "See. Even the food you prepare becomes play time. That's our silly mom, and we love you just like you are!"

Mom replied, "You are right. I love being creative, playing, and laughing. I love being the person God created me to be."

> **Today's Mom Step**
>
> Share a childhood passion with your family to let that little girl within you show.

You're My Favorite Child

Dear friends, let us love one another, for love is from God and every-one who loves is born of God and knows God. 1 JOHN 4:7

The woman who made the world laugh also made her children feel loved. Erma Bombeck saw the funny side of everyday life. She and her husband adopted a daughter, and then she gave birth to two sons.

She wrote a column called *I Always Loved You Best,* because that shared her unique love for each of her children. She shared the love of the first-born child as the first one to hold, the middle child who was easier as they were experienced parents, and his spot in life made him stronger, and the youngest for being the baby and happy with hand-me downs.

Erma lived her own quote, "When I stand before God at the end of my life, I would hope that I not have a single bit of talent left, and could say, I used everything you gave me." She found humor all around her and shared it joyfully. She appreciated mothers and supported equal rights for women. Erma wrote about the plight of women and serious topics like depression in ways that brought laughter and tears. Even during her kidney illness and cancer battle her humor remained.

Erma found strength in her natural optimistic outlook and humor. Moms do best when they use their natural strength and follow their passions. Being willing to laugh and see the lighter side of calamities is also a great way to release stress.

Her insights reflected her motherly love. In one popular column Erma described an imaginary conversation between an angel and God as the Lord created Eve. Toward the end of fashioning the mother, the angel noticed liquid on one cheek and stated, "There's a leak." God calmly replied, "It's a tear." God explained, "It's for joy, sadness, disappointment, pain, loneliness, and pride."

Today's Mom Step

Be willing to laugh in the midst of chaos and problems.

Taking a Break

Come to me, all you who are weary and burdened, and I will give you rest. MATTHEW 11:28

Mama turned off the stove, sat on the couch, and announced, "I'm giving everyone a little time to relax before dinner." That's how Ellen coped with anxiety that came during that time of day while she cooked, or later in life, when hot flashes or panic attacks would crop up.

Ellen sat for a few minutes, prayed silently, and then returned to finish dinner or sometimes asked one of the children to stir the pot, finish a salad, or other final task. She knew when she felt

GROWING A MOTHER'S HEART

overwhelmed, she had to pause, or else she might get cross or explode. Her children just thought that a little break in the midst of mom's activities was a normal part of life. She thanked God for children who accepted her need for timeouts.

For Ellen, medical issues and lower energy meant taking breaks and doing what she could. That didn't stop her from volunteering with a church drama group that involved the children, helping with their team sports, and assisting when her kids needed help with homework. She mentioned her little breaks to a girlfriend and expressed surprise when energetic Vickie said, "I need breaks too. I love how we get together and pray, and that's one way I distress, but I also need some physical activity to help me unwind."

Vickie explained, "I'm more likely to need to go on a run when hubby gets home to let off steam, but I love my long hot showers too." Ellen realized another friend took breaks by curling up with a good book. Another friend refreshed herself by meeting up with a friend and getting away from home for a little while. Another simply made a date with her husband to have a fun night out to enjoy a little romance. There are many ways to unwind and de-stress.

> **Today's Mom Step**
> Schedule breaks and allow yourself to calm down as needed.

Week 14
Mom-Strength
and Courage

Prayer for Strength to Support My Children

Lord, your word reminds me to be courageous and not fear. I had the strength to have this baby. I want the courage to face each day's challenges, the strength to get through difficult days, and the courage to be the mom my children need. Give me that courage and help me let go of fear. Let me draw on my strengths and lean on you in my weaknesses.

Help me be brave enough to volunteer and not worry that I'll let someone down. Help me have the courage to admit my mistakes and ask for forgiveness. When a crisis comes, let me trust you and hear your voice guiding me every step of the way.

Give me the courage to advocate for my children. I want to support their needs as they are young. Help me to also let my children speak up for themselves as they grow, so they might defend their faith and beliefs.

Let me also give my children a sense of adventure and courage to try new things and face their fears too. Let me model courage for my children and remind them that we can do all things with you and the strength you give us.

Wisdom from Future Moms

When I don't do my work, I don't get a reward, and mom gets angry at me for not even trying.

I can tell when Mom is angry: she uses my first and middle names.

Downhill without Brakes

Have I not commanded you? Be strong and courageous! Do not tremble or be dismayed, for the Lord your God is with you wherever you go. JOSHUA 1:9

Kitty drove to the preschool to drop off her children. As she started down a steep hill, her brakes gave way. The car headed straight for the fence and ocean. She prayed, "Lord, guide me in what to do. I trust you. I can't save all of us if we go over the edge."

Kitty heard a small voice in her head say, "Make that right turn and turn off the ignition." She turned the wheel sharply, praying no one was coming in the other direction. Then she turned the key, the engine died, and the car slowed down. She sat back, trembling, and closed her eyes.

Her oldest son called out, "Mom, what's the big idea? This isn't my school."

She laughed, and that helped her to stop shaking from the scare. She turned and said, "Our car broke down. I need to put it on the grass. We'll catch the shuttle when it comes." She turned the car back on and glided it onto the grass.

Her sons jumped up and down on the grass watching for the bus to come. They waved their arms, and the driver stopped. Kitty explained that the brakes stopped working, and they needed to get on although this was not a normal stop. He dropped them off at the school. Kitty called her husband, who came and slowly drove the car to a mechanic.

Kitty said to her husband, "I can't believe I had brakes go out twice in my life. As a teen I drove home on our very flat street and could not slow the car to turn into the driveway. I turned the car off, and I pulled onto the curb as it slowed down. I felt more scared with our little boys in the backseat as the car sped down-hill. I prayed and listened to what God whispered in my head."

Her husband hugged her, "Everyone is safe. God gave you strength and wisdom."

Today's Mom Step

In a crisis turn to God for strength and listen for wisdom.

Ruth, A Woman of Courage (Biblical Mom)

Ruth said, "Do not urge me to leave you or turn back from following you; for where you go, I will go, and where you lodge, I will lodge. Your people shall be my people, and your God, my God." RUTH 1:16

A strong commitment takes courage. Ruth, a poor widow in the old Testament, chose to follow her widowed mother-in-law Naomi to Israel. This meant leaving her home and going to a new place where she would be a stranger. With no money and no means of support the choice meant a life of poverty. She chose to trust the God of Naomi, the God she met through knowing her mother-in-law.

Once in Bethlehem, Ruth asked Naomi for permission to go and glean in a wheat field that belonged to a relative. Gleaning meant picking up the leftover stalks of wheat after the workers harvest a field. It's hard work to pick up enough golden stalks of wheat and fallen kernels to feed two women. Once home, she'd have to thrash the wheat by hand to release the edible kernels. She chose to do this through manual labor. The owner of the field noticed her and spoke kindly to her.

Ruth replied, "Why have I found favor in your sight that you should take notice of me, since I am a foreigner?" Boaz responded that he knew about her kindness to Naomi and her choice to come with her to a place she didn't know.

Ruth continued to accept and follow Naomi's advice. That led to her marriage to Boaz, freedom form poverty, and the birth of a son named Obed. Ruth's great-grandson David became the most beloved king of Israel and ancestor of Jesus. Ruth's courage and faith brought great blessings.

> **Today's Mom Step**
> Choose to be courageous and do something new.

Driving Lessons

The wheels were called in my hearing, the whirling wheels. EZEKIEL 10:13

Amanda sucked in her breath and said, "Okay. Turn on the key and let the engine start. Keep your foot on the brake." She wondered why she agreed to teach her son to drive a manual transmission car. He complained that dad made it too hard. The car jerked forward and stalled. Amanda chatted about the right amount of foot pressure and how to let up on the clutch easy.

They continued to bump and jerk. With each jerk, Amanda held her breath and wondered how she would ever let him on a real road. This seldom used dirt road seemed hard enough, although very safe with no other cars around. She thought, "This is one of the hardest things I've ever had to do. I've got to get through it." She switched places and demonstrated again. She looked at her son and saw him clenching the steering wheel. She said, "I know this seems hard and a bit scary, but you'll be okay. Pause for a moment, take a deep breath, and start again." When she focused on her son, she forgot to be scared. She realized that focusing on her children in difficult times always kept her from feeling afraid, because she just thought of what each one needed.

GROWING A MOTHER'S HEART

Her son got that license, and each time he picked up the keys she held her breath for a minute. One day, he came in and said, "Mom, I'm stuck. I didn't pull dad's car in straight and I can't back it up. Dad won't be happy." They went out, and she saw how close it came to the edge of the garage door opening, almost scraping it. She told him to get his younger brother. She took off the break. Then she said to her sons, "The car is little, so let's lift it and move it a little bit sideways. They all lifted and pushed. They did it! She could breathe easy again, until the next call-for-mom courage was needed.

> **Today's Mom Step**
> When you are scared when teaching your kids, think of your child, and you'll find courage.

Steadfast Dolley Madison (Historic Mom)

Be strong, and let us show ourselves courageous for the sake of our people and for the cities of our God; and may the Lord *do what is good in His sight.* 2 Samuel 10:12

Widowed with the loss of one son to yellow fever, Dolley struggled to raise her toddler alone. She sued her brother-in-law, the executor of her husband's estate, for a small sum of money due her. Then she remarried a year later. Her new husband, James Madison, served as a congressman in the newly formed U.S. government. After several years, James retired, and they moved to his farm in Virginia. When President Jefferson asked James to serve as Secretary of State, they moved to Washington D.C., where Dolley believed that entertaining would be important. She assisted widowed President Jefferson with White House social events.

James Madison become president after Jefferson, As First Lady, Dolley became famous for her social parties at the White

House, where her charm helped avert a diplomatic crisis and also made her husband a popular president. During the War of 1812 when the British approached the White House, Dolley hurried to preserve the White House papers and portrait of George Washington. She filled her carriage with the papers and sacrificed her personal possessions, putting the country first.

Dolley's son Payne Todd never found a career and struggled with alcoholism and numerous stints in jail for various shootings and disturbing the peace. At one point, Payne went to debtor's prison. Dolley and James, now retired from the presidency, mortgaged half of their estate to rescue him. After the death of James, the government hired Dolley to organize and copy her husband's papers. That work saved her from poverty. Dolley remained devoted to her son and worked hard to support both of them since he could not control his alcoholism or gambling and failed at all his endeavors to earn money. She rose to every challenge as a woman and a mother at a time when people did not understand addictions or offer programs to help.

Today's Mom Step

Remain strong when children make poor choices and find programs to help them.

Brokenness

Restore to me the joy of Your salvation and sustain me with a willing spirit. PSALM 51:12

Mary hung up the phone, curled up in a ball, and cried. A man had called to ask how she could let her husband have an affair with his wife. Her first reaction of nausea ended in vomiting. She later confronted her husband, who admitted it and shared about his other affairs. This began her divorce journey and brokenness of her family. Asking questions only brought more pain as she learned more of her husband's years of unfaithfulness. She prayed and clung to a few scriptures that she repeated over and over. She journaled throughout her journey.

Her husband tried to turn their children against her and finally had a family meeting. He listed all the bad things he could say about their mom including many lies and declared, "She's an unfit wife and mom." Mary sat quietly stunned and just prayed for God's peace and joy.

Her children hugged their mother and responded, "Mom's my rock." And "I'm with mom." That enraged her husband.

After several difficult months, they divorced. God blessed Mary and the children with all they needed. Throughout Mary's first part of the journey, she prayed for God to restore joy to her broken heart. He gave her a picture in her mind of a little box that opened to shine light everywhere. That represented joy overflowing. Then as the struggle escalated, and her children felt hurt, she prayed for peace and for the Lord to protect her children's hearts from bitterness. She continued to work and provide for the family and to show love and live what she read in the Bible.

> **Today's Mom Step**
> Ask for God's peace every day and be ready to trust him when bad news hits your family.

Her teen son grew angry and pulled away from God, while her daughter drew closer to God. Mary continues to pray for her son and for him to have peace.

Week 15

Perchance to Sleep

Prayer for Enough Rest

Dear Lord, as a mom I understand exhaustion and tiredness more than ever. The mountains of clothes and dishes, the toys covering all the spaces in the house, and the handprints on the walls never end. Help me remember that smiles, cuddles, and giggles also never end, and let those perk me up.

It seems I barely lay my head down when a cry or a hand tugging on me wakes me up again. Your grace is sufficient for me, so also let the sleep you give me be sufficient. Let fifteen minutes refresh me as much as several hours.

Also help my sister-moms who are tired and refresh them too. Help us share joys to lift up one another. These are blessed years but also busy days when it's easy to get overwhelmed and tired.

Help me not be anxious when my head touches the pillow and trust you will guide me each day to make the right choices for my children so I can drift off peacefully.

Wisdom from Future Moms

Now I know why mom is so tired; she's the Fairy God mother! (after a little girl caught her mom putting money under her pillow when she lost a tooth)

What makes my mom so tired is ME.

I can't close my eyes. I'm broken. I'm going to snore just a little bit.

Sleeping Mommy

In peace I will both lie down and sleep, for You alone, O Lord, make me to dwell in safety. PSALM 4:8

Robin's friend Jan visited with her daughter. The next morning Robin said, "Jan you look so tired. Did your daughter wake you up last night?"

Jan replied, "No, your daughter did?"

"Mine? I didn't hear her. What happened?"

"All night long she'd wake up, cry, and made noises. Each time I went and stood by the door, but then she'd go back to sleep. How does she wake you up?

"She shakes the crib a little bit."

That night Jan decided she would not get up for Robin's daughter. At one point it sounded like a train barreling by and she jumped up. She watched Robin half asleep go in and pick up her daughter. She had also seen Robin's little girl using all her strength to shake the crib back and forth.

Robin sounded surprised by the description in the morning. Over the years as Robin had more babies, she realized she and her husband are among a group of parents who sleep through their babies crying at night. No wonder her little ones all shook the crib. One crib collapsed as she lifted a son out of it, and another son started handing her rails that came loose as he shook the crib. They all walked at young ages, from seven to nine months old, were switched to beds, and then went to her during the night. Robin ended her days so tired, she simply collapsed and slept soundly. Her happy babies all survived.

Today's Mom Step

Let your baby cry a little while during the night to see if he or she will fall back to sleep.

Stressed out Mama (Biblical Mom: A Widow and Elijah)

So she said to Elijah, "What do I have to do with you, O man of God? You have come to me to bring my iniquity to remembrance and to put my son to death!" 1 KINGS 17:18

Stress, grief, fear, and other emotions can prevent a person from sleeping. God sent help to one woman in the Old Testament who faced great stress.

During a famine and drought, God sent Elijah the prophet to Zarephath to find a widow who would provide for him. When Elijah met the woman and asked her for bread, she responded with her dismal news, "I have no bread, only a handful of flour in the bowl and a little oil in the jar; and behold, I am gathering a few sticks that I may go in and prepare for me and my son, that we may eat it and die."

She wanted to give her son the last bit of comfort possible, a small meal. Elijah told her not to be afraid and that her jar of flour and jar of oil would not run out until the drought ended. God had sent Elijah to perform a miracle for this widow that she could see and enjoy daily, with every bite she chewed. Elijah stayed in her home.

Later, after the drought ended, she faced her son's near death from sickness, and she cried out in despair to Elijah. She asked if he came to point out her sins and take her son. She forgot past miracles as she watched her son slowly dying. Elijah took the boy out of her arms, laid him on a bed, prayed, and stretched himself out over the

> **Today's Mom Step**
> Under stress, no matter how small or great, pray for God's help.

boy three times. This revived the child, and Elijah carried the boy to his mother and called out, "Look! Your child is alive!" Her emotional roller coaster ended with joy.

The woman praised Elijah and God and stated she now knew God spoke through him.

Sleepless Children

The Lord called yet again, "Samuel!" So Samuel arose and went to Eli and said, "Here I am, for you called me." But he answered, "I did not call, my son, lie down again. 1 Samuel 3:6

If children can't sleep, then mama cannot sleep. Donna's son came and kept patting her shoulder until he woke her

"I had a bad dream, Mommy, and I'm scared."

Donna tried to calm him down and send him back to bed, but he would not budge alone. She had just gotten his little sister back to bed. She got up, tucked him in, and turned to leave.

"No, mommy, don't go. I'm too afraid."

Donna thought, "It's hard enough getting him to bed the first time with the endless pleas for a drink, to go to the bathroom, or another story. I seem to settle one down, and then another wakes up. I think they are in cahoots with one another, and each one takes a different hour."

Donna sat beside him, gently rubbing his back until he drifted off. She headed back to bed. Alas, her older daughter came in and said, "All the noise woke me up. I need a drink." Donna handed her a little bottle of water she had put beside her bed just in case this happened.

Donna looked at the clock. She'd have to get up for the day in two hours and had hardly slept a wink. She prayed for God to give her rest, and 2 Corinthians 2:19 popped into her mind, "My grace is sufficient for you." She thought, Lord, I know your grace is sufficient, but please can your rest be sufficient too?" Soon she drifted off to sleep.

In the morning her son raced in and yelled, "Mom, I need breakfast!"

Donna got up and felt re-freshed. All day she felt ener-gized. She remembered ask-ing God if His rest was also enough and smiled. She'd pray that scripture before bed and trust God.

> **Today's Mom Step**
> Trust your sleep to God and ask for the sleep time you get to be refreshing.

War and Sleepless Nights (Historic Mom)

I have been in labor and hardship, through many sleepless nights, in hunger and thirst, often without food, in cold and exposure. 2 CORINTHIANS 11:27

Stress infringed on the sleep of the beautiful red-haired Baron-ess Fredericka Reidesel. She chose to follow her husband to America as he assisted the British in the American Revolution. She brought antiques with her to sell along the way to cover their expenses.

As a child, Frederika and her family accompanied her dad to battlefields, so she understood many of the perils. She wanted to be with her husband and chose to go to America with him. She cared for her children during the voyage as they suffered from seasickness. Once they arrived, she often loss sleep since battles separated her from the Baron, and she worried about his life.

During the Battle of Saratoga, she and her children stayed in a house where at least eleven cannon balls struck and passed through the walls. She stayed there and ministered to wounded soldiers. When she sat, her children laid their heads on her lap.

She gave away scraps of food she found to the wounded men, and her children but ate little herself. The soldiers called her an angel of comfort. She slept very little for six days until the British surrendered. Then her family became prisoners until the war ended.

They were brought to the American camp, where the soldier's compassion surprised her. General Burgoyne treated her and her children to a meal in his tent and then invited her family with her husband to his home. For a few years they lived in various areas as captives but always received good treatment where she also found rest. Eventually they returned to their own country, and Frederika published her account of their time in America.

Mom Lesson at the Zoo

But now ask the beasts and let them teach you; and the birds of the heavens, and let them tell you. JOB 12:7

Debbie Wilson's second child had colic and couldn't sleep before 4:00 a.m. Her two-year-old was at her bed greeting her with a cheery "Good morning, Mommy!" by 6:15 a.m. Debbie felt exhausted but believed she needed to soldier on and accomplish tasks when they napped.

Debbie took her children to the zoo in the spring to see the baby animals. They had a difficult time seeing many animals because they were all napping. And guess what? Their mothers napped with their babies. Bears and tigers and even monkeys settled down to snuggle together and sleep. Moms and babes all looked so peaceful. She snapped photos of animals sleeping.

She wondered where she got the idea to maintain her former schedule when children came instead of giving herself permission to rest when they rested. The mothers at the zoo showed more wisdom than she had with her babies. It's God's example for us to let go of work and rest. It's an act of faith to choose to snatch a nap with kids instead of using the time to work.

The next afternoon, Debbie gathered their stuffed animals and children for a nap with her. She reminded them how the animals napped. She discovered that cuddling up with her little ones for napping felt great, and she drifted off easily.

> **Today's Mom Step**
> Set a timer and take a short nap while your children nap.

She woke up energized and did chores as they snacked. Then she suggested that since they napped together, her daughter could sort laundry with her too. Her little girl giggled and helped. As they folded clothes, they made animal noises and talked about the trip to the zoo.

Week 16

Creating a Haven

Prayer for Our Home to Be a Haven

Dear Lord, I'm thankful for my family and home. Help me make our home a haven so children feel safe and accepted there. Let us have open doors to welcome visitors and make them feel at home too. Let our home be a place we love to come together to play, talk, and work. Let it be a welcoming place for visitors where we can share our faith and show love and hospitality to all who enter.

Help me keep our home organized and yet comfortable. Help me inspire my family to cooperate in caring for the home. Let me find a system that works to keep down the continual battle with clutter.

Bless our home and protect it from negative influences. Protect us from intruders so we might dwell in safety. Fill it with your love and peace. Let us live together in harmony.

Wisdom from Future Moms

I wish my mom would let me have a puppy. She says she has enough work with me in the house.

"Awwwww!!!! So cute!" said whenever one little girl catches her mom and dad, cuddling on the couch, watching tv.

Pretzels and Guests

Do not neglect to show hospitality to strangers, for by this some have entertained angels without knowing it. HEBREWS 13:2

Midafternoon, Sally measured and poured flour and other ingredients into the bread machine and hit the dough button. The pretzel dough would be ready when teens started showing up. Her children's friends usually came over after swim team and track practice and stayed for dinner. To stretch the food and help visitors feel welcome, she started a routine. As each teen arrived, she assigned each a task in making the pretzels or breadsticks from shaping the dough to brushing on oil and sprinkling on toppings. Others helped set the table, another opportunity to share with the visitors on how to prepare for a meal.

As the guys and gals chatted and worked, Sally wove in a few things about dinner when someone new showed up. Sally used the time of cooking to share how to pass the food, wait for the blessing, and other meal routines her family observed. By the time they sat, everyone felt like part of the family. Her husband said the blessing and started asking about each person's day, going around the table clockwise. He listened and added humorous comments or words of encouragement. For repeat visitors, he'd ask a question about what had happened concerning a past problem or accomplishment they'd discussed.

> **Today's Mom Step**
> Keep supplies on hand to make a quick treat for visitors.

Visitors enjoyed the meals and especially loved the breads they helped make. They'd thank Sally and a new visitor often add, "It's so much better to be here than eating a TV dinner or leftovers alone at home. It always feels like you really care." Another commented, "I don't have to study for the SAT, because the conversation enriches my vocabulary." Sally hugged each person as they prepared to leave and invited them to return.

A Baby in the Temple (Biblical Woman, Jehosheba)

But Jehosheba, the daughter of King Joram, sister of Ahaziah, took Joash the son of Ahaziah and stole him from among the king's sons who were being put to death, and placed him and his nurse in the bedroom. So they hid him from Athaliah, and he was not put to death. 2 KINGS 11:2

Joash started his life in a palace. When his father, King Ahaziah died, the king's mother wanted the throne. She decided to have all the king's children killed so no one could take the crown from her. But one woman secretly defied her. Jehosheba, the king's sister, kidnapped Joash and hid him and his nurse.

Jehosheba hid Joash in a bedroom and then in the temple for six years. The little boy lived in hiding, no longer in a fancy palace, but probably in a little room within the temple. His aunt kept him safe in God's house under the watchful care of Jehoiada the priest. When Joash turned seven, Jehoiada revealed his presence to the captains of the army. He shared a plan to place Joash on the throne as the true king. When that day came, they crowned the young king in the temple and called the people to celebrate. When his evil grandmother heard the noise, she investi-

> **Today's Mom Step**
>
> Keep your children safe from evil. Be surrounding them with God's presence. Keep your home free from movies, books, and language that are not wholesome.

gated. She saw Joash and tore her clothes. The priest had her removed and put to death. Joash once again lived in the palace. He served as a good king while Jehoiada lived and counseled him. He repaired the temple. He led the people in spiritual renewal once they found the lost Book of the Law written by Moses.

Jehosheba risked her life to keep Joash safe. She placed him in a safe haven, in God's presence that he needed most, in a place that helped break the chain of evil in the palace, at least for a time. We don't see his mother, but we see how his aunt served as a true mother.

Bug Out

By wisdom a house is built, and by understanding it is established.
PROVERBS 24:3

Beth woke up with itchy red marks on her body. She quickly discovered bedbugs had come to visit. With tight finances she tried home remedies to no avail. Her spouse and children helped vacuum, clean, and bag up cloth items. Finally, she gave up and hired someone who rid the home of the nasty critters in mere hours.

However, the problem had transformed their home life from a place where friends dropped into to a place people avoided. Beth explained the problem had ended, but fear kept people away. It took weeks for family members to relax at home and feel comfortable going to bed. She realized that if she felt uncomfortable in her home it would be hard for friends to relax. As the mom, she wanted her children to be happy and that meant remaking their home into a place people wanted to visit.

Beth planned a friendship party as an open house. Everyone enjoyed her husband's great cooking, and she planned a tasting party to try new recipes. She bought new pillows and freshened

GROWING A MOTHER'S HEART

the home with flowers and little touches. Her family made signs with welcoming scriptures and pulled out popular games. They had an afternoon time for the kids to have friends play games and enjoy the treats. Evenings were reserved for their adult friends.

Today's Mom Step

Do a welcome check of your home to be sure visitors will feel comfortable.

Friends who came raved about the food and asked for the recipes. They decided to plan some regular gatherings again. Over the next few days, the doorbell rang several times as friends dropped by to visit. She continued to make sure both her family and visitors felt safe, comfy, and welcomed.

Harriet Tubman, a Modern Day Moses (Historic Mom)

And they sang the song of Moses, the bond-servant of God, and the song of the Lamb, saying, "Great and marvelous are Your works, O Lord God, the Almighty; Righteous and true are Your ways, King of the nations!" REVELATION 15:3

Called a modern-day Moses during the 1800s, Harriet Tubman led at least seventy slaves into the haven of the Underground Railroad. Harriet suffered lashings often, and once a man threw a two-pound weight on her head that resulted in a lifetime of seizures, migraines, and narcoleptic episodes.

After Harriet escaped from the Maryland plantation to Pennsylvania, she worked to free others and extended the underground railroad to Canada. That brought her people to safety from laws requiring the return of escaped slaves to their owners.

Once freed, Harriet said, "The sun came like gold through the trees, and I felt like I was in heaven." Harriet trusted God, spoke to Him as a friend, and shared her faith with others. She found herself a stranger in a strange land but resolved to work and save money to free her people. She found work and used her funds and connections she made in the underground railroad to help slaves escape to freedom. She freed her parents, niece Margaret, and several siblings. She used songs to communicate since laws forbid them to gather and talk.

After the war, Harriet lived in Auburn, New York. She supported herself by selling produce she grew, pigs she raised, while taking in borders. Her first husband, John Tubman, died in 1867. She later married a Civil War veteran, Nelson Davis, and they adopted a girl named Gertie. She served as a model of love and faith to her daughter. One great-great niece Deidre said she hoped people remember Harriet as a woman of God who wanted freedom for all people.

> **Today's Mom Step**
>
> Be inventive in reaching your goals and follow your passions, especially ones that help others.

Let Go of Chaos

For God is not a God of disorder but of peace, as in all the meetings of God's holy people. 1 CORINTHIANS 14:33 (NLT)

Sandra Felton trembled as she picked up the phone and dialed the plumber. How could she let him in her home piled with junk? The clutter covered every corner and cranny. She thought, "I cannot not live like this anymore. My children, husband, and I deserve better."

She sought help and found very little in books and advice. She started with one corner of the front room. Each day she spent an hour cleaning up the clutter. She filled trash bags of garbage and boxes of donations she gave to a place that would pick up her unwanted items.. Sandra decided to group things and get each type into one place with office supplies in the den, crafts in a cupboard, and sporting equipment in the garage. She quickly realized she needed the family to get onboard.

As each person entered and dropped a coat or book, she sent them back to pick things up and shared where the items now belonged. She chatted at dinner about how things were improving, and, with their help, the home could stay much nicer. She snapped photos of her organized home and suggested the kids invite friends over and she'd provide some snacks.

A few months later she looked around and noticed the house was again building up clutter due to a lack of rules to maintain the home. So, no dinner until they cleaned clutter from the living spaces, and she scheduled a weekly time for organizing. Since the home looked clean but plain, she added artwork and touches that made colors pop. Flowers as themes for accents and decorations added beauty. From there Sandra created an organization to help people around the world go from messy to organized with beauty.

> **Today's Mom Step**
> Choose one area that collects clutter and make a change to get that more organized.

Week 17

Where's My Support?

Prayer for a Strong Support Network

Lord thank you for blessing me with family and for being with me in the journey as a mom. I cannot do it all alone. I also need support. Help me find the right mentors when I need advice. Help me find mom friends to walk with me and share our joys and struggles. Help me find authentic friends to ease the stress with laughter and release anxiety with assurance that I'm not alone. Bless those friends too. Let me pray for them and listen to their needs too.

Lord, thanks for mom groups, family, and friends who care. Help me appreciate the support they offer. Guide me to accept the support gratefully and the wisdom to know what voices to listen to and follow.

Help me inspire my spouse and children to support my efforts as a mom. Let me encourage and appreciate each one so they will want to respond with love. Help me build the bonds, so we will encourage and support one another. Let me accept and show gratitude for all the big and little hands that help in my home and life. Their help shows they appreciate my efforts.

Wisdom from Future Moms

Most fun thing about mom is doing activities with her or relaxing with her after a hard day.

My mom doesn't know how to use the dishwasher! We have to do it for her!

Where's My Neighbor?

Now we who are strong ought to bear the weaknesses of those without strength and not just please ourselves. ROMANS 15:1

Megan emailed the neighbors with a request to help make meals for one of the families who had a child in the hospital. Everyone started filling in the group calendar of what they'd make and when. Whether a new baby, someone needing help with a project, or an unexpected problem, the neighbors all pitched in. Casey discovered they'd moved to the best community and enjoyed the young families although their children were grown. She often signed up. Her husband Jim picked up his shovel or saw and lent a hand when someone needed a yard overhaul.

When the doctor shared the news of her husband's cancer, Casey shared it with a neighbor. They didn't need immediate help, but neighbors responded to needs—even ones not expressed. When Casey mentioned it might be better to switch the den furniture with an upstairs spare bedroom's furniture so Jim would not have to climb stairs, neighbors repainted the den, and some of the men came and quickly moved all the furniture. Various men came and sat with her husband so Casey could run errands or enjoy a girls' night out.

Casey still made meals for other families in need and even gave comfort to friends who faced bad news. When her children visited to see their dad, neighbors brought over food. The young children in the neighborhood loved to make chocolates or pretzels at her house and still did that too. They would ask, "How is Mr. Jim was doing?"

> **Today's Mom Step**
> Do something kind for a neighbor.

One neighbor said, "I love watching how the two of you face this battle. You give me strength."

When Jim passed away, neighbors helped in countless ways with yard work, fixing a broken toilet, and stopping by to chat.

Baby Connections (Biblical Moms, Elizabeth and Mary)

For behold, when the sound of your greeting reached my ears, the baby leaped in my womb for joy. LUKE 1:44

Two preggy women greeted one another with great joy. They rejoiced for one another. Elizabeth, a woman too old to think she'd be a mother, would soon have a son. Mary, young and engaged, didn't expect to have this baby before her wedding. But God chose each one for a special purpose.

The angel Gabriel told Mary that God chose her to be the mother of the promised savior and Mary accepted. She remained a virgin, as the Holy Spirit brought life into her womb. Gabriel had also spoken to Elizabeth's husband Zacharias to inform him that they would have a son. This child would be filled with God's Holy Spirit even in the womb and would prepare people's hearts for the Lord. All the angel said came to pass.

Elizabeth's baby leapt in the presence of the baby in Mary's womb, and the Holy Spirit filled Elizabeth. These two women understood the significance of one another's baby. The older woman praised Mary for her role as mother of the Savior and expressed how honored she felt that Mary came to visit her. Mary came to serve Elizabeth and help her prepare for the birth of John the Baptist, the one who would prepare people for her own son. She called Mary blessed for her faith that God would fulfill His promise to their people through her. Mary praised God. She stayed for three months. What joy filled the home, as these women of faith shared the excitement of becoming mothers.

They probably made baby clothes together and chatted about their hopes and growing love for the little ones yet unseen. They shared hope for their families and also for their people knowing they were in the presence of the promised Savior.

Mom Groups!

To sum up, all of you be harmonious, sympathetic, brotherly, kindhearted, and humble in spirit. 1 PETER 3:8

Another military move, and this time with a six-month-old baby. This stint would keep them in one place for two years for her husband's graduate studies. He quickly found in the Coast Guard several classmates from his academy days and introduced Susan to them. She found some support there, and they experienced a deepened friendship with one couple they already knew from college days. They started getting together weekly and scheduled playdates for their daughters.

At the community playground, Susan met neighbors and joined their Bible study group. Wow! The little ones, all about the same age, made fast friends. They could meet up daily at the playground or the little lake nearby to let the children run and play.

Susan also spotted a notice of a church co-op where she could take turns with babysitting and also meet up with moms. She stopped in to chat and discover more about the group. Her daughter made a beeline for the play kitchen area. An older woman introduced herself as the organizer and shared how they worked. This loving woman seemed full of information but waited to be asked before giving any advice. At story time, the woman shared about Jesus with the children. Susan signed up for time slots to help and took the number to call in when she might need a sitter.

> **Today's Mom Step**
> Appreciate the groups you're in and look to see if there's a mom you can ask to join.

Susan had her morning coffee group at the playground and also met with some lovely mentor moms at the church co-op. She and her husband developed friendships with couples to have fun together. Finding the right groups made life there such a joy and so hard to leave a few years later. She moved on, knowing the first thing to do after unpacking was to find a few support groups.

Inspiring Others to Lend Support (Historic Mom, Eleanor Roosevelt)

Let us consider how to stimulate one another to love and good deeds. HEBREWS 10:24

As a mom, Eleanor's heart cried for these women. She toured factories with her husband, President Franklin Roosevelt, and while the men showed their progress at making planes, ships, and more, she looked at the women and heard children cry through open windows.

Women with husbands away worked to help the war effort and to feed their families. They had no one to care for their children so they left them in cars with open windows and parked near the open factory windows. They used their breaks to tend to the needs of their sons and daughters. She spoke to many of the women and discovered they had to skip work to shop for groceries because shelves emptied by the later part of the day. They drove miles to get to work, so banks closed before they arrived home.

Eleanor met with the factory leaders and shared her plan. She wanted them to hire top educators, nurses, and dieticians to plan and establish daycare centers on their premises to help the women. Within a few months, plants around the country opened daycare centers. The morale increased and so did the output. The women smiled more, and their children enjoyed making friends, doing art, and learning to read.

Eleanor also pushed to have hours staggered, banks to have more flexible hours, and encouraged factory owners to hire shoppers to take orders in the morning and deliver groceries at the end of the shifts.

As a mother herself, the First Lady understood these mothers worked hard to support their families. She listened, noticed needs, and found support for women and their children.

Support Partner

Therefore encourage one another and build up one another, just as you also are doing. 1 THESSALONIANS 5:11

Connie and Myrna chatted. They volunteered for the same organization. Myrna said "We're both trying to get back into our careers now that our children are getting older. How would you like to be my support partner? We could pray for each other and also listen and encourage each other in our careers."

Connie sounded excited to try it. They agreed to meet once a month at a restaurant halfway between their homes. Connie had started a small business, and Myrna wrote articles and books. They shared the ups and downs of their work as well as family concerns and joys. They prayed. They also took time to laugh. It helped them each forge ahead. Over the years, they also supported one another, as they each raised their children and became empty nesters and then caregivers and widows.

Neither thought her career would have succeeded without the other's support. Myrna inspired Connie to start speaking and contact complimentary businesses that could help her business grow. Connie inspired Myrna to speak to local and then state groups. Myrna helped Connie pack and move when she downsized. Connie, a photographer, took headshots for Myrna. They rejoiced that their support partnership lasted for so many years and that the friendship became so strong.

> **Today's Mom Step**
> Find a support partner and commit to listening and praying for her.

When they each moved further away, and Connie retired and remarried they stopped meeting but remained friends. When Myrna traveled near Connie's home, she stayed with her for a few days to catch up.

Week 18

How Can I Calm

My Anxious Heart?

A Mother's Prayer on Anxious Days

Lord, please calm my anxious heart. Let my mind dwell on joy and the smiles of my children. I want so much for my precious children to know you and to experience your love. Every morning as I hear their steps I smile. Every smile takes away my breathe and lights up my day.

And yet, I fret each day. I look and wonder if my child will have good and worthy friends, learn well enough to succeed, and trust you. I hear bad news and worry that trouble will come. I see obstacles in the path and fear my little one will stumble and fall.

Then I remember that I learn when I fall, and you protect me when trouble comes. You will do this for my child too. Once again, today, I entrust my child's safety and life to you. I will treasure all the days you give us. You created and love my precious child even more than I do. Thank you for the gift of my child's life and every day you give us to share.

Calm my anxiety about finances and the future too. Help me remember that you care for the sparrows and will care for me. Help me laugh at the future, knowing you are in charge.

Wisdom from Future Moms

I wish moms knew to take care of children nicely.

When one little child noticed her mom looking sad, she would press her head against her mom's forehead, open her big brown eyes wide, and say, *"Don't be sad."*

Left Behind

As they were returning, after spending the full number of days, the boy Jesus stayed behind in Jerusalem. But His parents were unaware of it. Luke 2:43

"What do you mean he's not in the car?" Karli yelled.

Karli had already done a U-turn and returned home to get that son's forgotten costume for the school event but couldn't believe that she left him behind.

Michael said, "When you went inside to get Jaime's costume, he ran inside too."

Karli pulled over, looked in the back, and checked under the seats. She only counted two heads. And four feet.

She drove the rest of the way to school. Michel jumped out. Darlene held her box costume covered with yellow feathers from several feather dusters and asked, "How can I be little bird without my big bird?"

"I'll go get the big bird. Go into your class." She'd continue driving in circles.

Back home, Karli found Jaime sitting on the front steps. He walked over and hopped in."

She wanted to scream and ask him why he disobeyed and got out of the car but held her tongue. She asked, "Were you afraid when you saw we had left?"

"No. You came back for my costume, so I knew you'd come back for me." Her child's trust melted her heart and her panic dissolved.

We sometimes mess up, but leaving a child behind makes us feel we should be labeled *Neglectful Mom of the*

> ### Today's Mom Step
> Take time to notice what your children are doing and trust that God is always with each little one.

Year. Our children trust us so completely, and yet we can be forgetful in many ways. We can overlook their needs or words. In our busyness we must be mindful. They need us to be with them fully.

Mary's Anxiety (Biblical Mom, Mary, Mother of Jesus)

When they saw Him, they were astonished; and His mother said to Him, "Son, why have You treated us this way? Behold, Your father and I have been anxiously looking for You." LUKE 2:48

He's missing! Mary, the mother of Jesus lost her son. She and Joseph searched everywhere starting with family and friends. They retraced their steps. They may have feared that Jesus would be anxious too. Instead. the scene at the temple astonished them when they saw Him teaching leaders. Mary questioned His actions and expressed her fear.

At twelve (the age of Jesus then), our children feel grown and make choices without our knowledge. They expect us to understand and not worry.

Like Mary, we have mother's hearts. We worry. Her anxiety must have grown larger over the three days of hunting for her precious child. She may have choked each time she asked if anyone had seen Jesus as she rushed through the streets of Jerusalem. They had gone to the temple to celebrate the Passover and worship God. Within hours they forgot to trust Him.

Mary revealed her heart. Jesus reacted calmly. He expected they would know to find Him in the temple, His Father's house. As God, Jesus knew that angels had revealed His identity to Mary and Joseph before His birth. As parents, they reacted from love and fear.

This glimpse of Mary reassures us that fear for our child's safety is natural. The response Jesus made caused Mary to ponder and remember. We echo her fears when our child causes us anxiety as we think, "Why did you do this? Didn't you know we'd be afraid?"

How often do we recall the times we think we failed or wonder over words our children spoke? Deep in our hearts we store memories, laughter, and tears of the years along with hope.

Sleeping Beauty

And behold, there arose a great storm on the sea, so that the boat was being covered with the waves; but Jesus Himself was asleep. MATTHEW 8:24

Katy dozed off and woke with a start. She checked on the baby, and then called her tiny two-year-old daughter to come. She heard no response. She searched every room but could not find her little girl. She raced outside and checked the yard. She went inside, picked up her baby son, and started knocking on doors. No one had seen little Callie.

Another mom came over and also looked everywhere in the house. They checked closets, under beds, and behind curtains. Soon the neighbors all started passing the word and hunting for the little green-eyed blond girl wearing a bright red dress. Finally, one of her daughter's older friends came up and said, "I found her. Follow me. Shhh."

They tiptoed after Joey to the play kitchen set, and he opened the door of the stove to reveal her sleeping inside it. Katy lifted her daughter out and hugged her.

A friend blew a horn to let everyone know they found her child. People gathered around and laughed when they heard about the hiding spot while Callie rubbed her sleepy eyes and asked, "Why is everyone here? Is this a party?"

Her mom said, "I think we should celebrate that we have great neighbors. I made cookies this morning."

Children can be playful and find little spots to snuggle up. That can panic a mother while a little one enjoys an adventure. They can also sleep so soundly and peacefully that they do not hear us call. Thankfully caring neighbors respond to help.

> **Today's Mom Step**
>
> When you panic, pause, pray, breathe, calmly react, and also know who to call for help.

Good Out of the Worst Scenario! (Historic Mom, Diane Simone, Amber Alert System)

Casting all your anxiety on Him, because He cares for you.
1 PETER 5:7

One lost child opened the way for others to be found.

Amber biked to a parking lot, and only one person saw a man grab her off her bicycle and heard her scream as he shoved her in his truck. Her five-year-old brother Ricky rode his bicycle beside her but didn't understand what happened. Alas, five days later another stranger walking her dog spotted Amber's dead body floating in a creek.

Diane Simone, a mom herself, read the story and mourned for Donna, who had lost her child. Diane came up with a plan. She called a local radio station and asked if they could issue alerts for missing children similar to announcing weather alerts.

People at the station coordinated with the police to start the Amber Alert System in the Dallas-Ft. Worth area in 1996. Amber's initials stand for America's Missing: Broadcast Emergency Response. Such alerts signal a loss and remind us of a mother's fear. It's a call to pray. For many anxious mothers, the alerts have brought more than hope and have reunited them with their precious child.

Rae Leigh Bradbury, the first child saved from the Amber Alert, started college in 2017. Her mother described the anxious moments as "emptiness and I don't know what to do feeling." Ninety minutes later, a passerby spotted the infant.

Amber Alerts remind us to be aware. We might spot the clue to help another mother. When we are alert to what's happening, we can notice a mother's anxiety and pray with her.

> **Today's Mom Step**
>
> Remind children of safety rules around strangers who want to take them somewhere.

Lost Buddies

The eyes of the LORD are toward the righteous and His ears are open to their cry. PSALM 34:15

Bruce had his friend, Alex, over for a playdate. Both were quiet children and were known to play well together. On this occasion, the two of them started building with blocks while their moms, April and Trixie, sat to chat. Later, April and Trixie went to the kitchen to make some tea after reminding the boys to stay in the playroom.

After some time had passed, April and Trixie walked back to the playroom, but didn't see the boys. Trixie called out, "Are you hiding on us?" No answer came. Trixie then searched the house, the porch, the yard, and the neighborhood, shouting "Bruce! Alex!" Since they lived on a military base on a small island, Trixie called security, and the chief who answered asked for a description.

The moms described the outfits, and the man replied, "We got 'em here. Neither boy would say a word, but they sure liked the ice cream we offered them." The boys remembered the rule to not speak to strangers but forgot the rule to not go outside without an adult.

The women rushed over to the security gate and found out that someone found the boys hanging over the fence at the water's edge. They had wandered outside past the golf course, and down the hill. So, the moms raced over, picked up their stray children, and hugged them.

Back at April's house, they sat down and went over safety rules again with their boys. They explained that the boys did not have permission to leave the house. As the boys went back to playing, Trixie said, "I feel like a terrible mom. I had no clue my son left your house."

April replied, "Children can move fast. You're a great mom. It's so hard not to worry."

Trixie said, "You're a great mom too. I'm so thankful we had each other to face this escapade. And I'm thankful it

> **Today's Mom Step**
> Don't be distracted during a child's play date. If you have a home alarm system, set it when children are inside, so you'll know if one sneaks out.

ended fast." The two women hugged each other after a long, harrowing, yet humorous ordeal.

Week 19

Faithful Moms

Prayer for Unshakeable Faith

Dear Lord, I love you, and I'm thankful for your blessings and faith in me. Let me continue to grow closer to you and to grow in grace. May my faithfulness show my children how faith works in my life. You are my rock to keep me steady in hard times, a gentle hand to wipe my tears in time of sorrow, and the one who delights in me as I remain faithful.

Draw each of my children close to you, and may the fruit of the spirit be in them. Guide me to teach them the Bible stories and truths that will touch their hearts and grow their minds so they will be faithful to you.

I am thankful I can lean on you every moment, no matter what happens. I trust that you want what is best for me and my family. On days when I can only muster a mustard seed of faith, that is enough for you to move mountains. When my faith seems to overflow, then praises pour out and my heart sings. When evil strikes and disasters come, I will trust in you and not my circumstances. Through faith I see the world differently and know your power is mighty and forever.

Let my friends see my faith in my life so they will grow in faith too.

Wisdom from Future Moms

Mom prayed to meet a good man, and Dad came to church. I think he needed someone to pray for him.

Mom prays and reads the Bible in the morning. She says that's how she fills her tank to get through the day. Sometimes I think she needs to fill it again in the middle of the day.

What Did I Do Wrong?

That I may proclaim with the voice of thanksgiving and declare all Your wonders. PSALM 26:7

Amy felt so inadequate as a mom. She fretted that she did something wrong and should not have let her daughter take a certain medicine for strep throat. In 2017, Bella lost her voice and then the use of an arm, followed by paralysis and eventually, inability to walk. Amy's mother Mary and the rest of the family comforted Amy and said she did not do anything wrong. They made love cards that encouraged Amy with words like, "I loved it when you did _____. It made me feel so_____."

A few months later, Bella sat by the Christmas tree and wrote, "I want to sing."

Mary replied, "You can sing, and your heart and God will hear you."

"I want God to hear my voice." Mary went to prepare a snack for them, when she heard a whisper. She found Bella singing "Silent Night" in a whisper. Her voice began to return, and Bella started writing songs and singing at church. She also did art to make picture books of the songs.

Amy kept investigating what they could do for Bella and her sister Naomi, who became legally blind from medicines. She researched foods, therapy, and anything else to do for the girls—including detoxing efforts. Bella prayed and journaled. Caleb, the youngest child, started to homeschool with his sisters so he could serve his sisters and stop bringing home germs.

In 2018, Bella could use a walker a bit. At the start of

Today's Mom Step

Praise God when it's hard. Pray, trust His will, and make encouragement cards for any mom feeling inadequate.

GROWING A MOTHER'S HEART

2019, Bella Cardwell rejoiced and said it was her best year because she had learned to hear God's voice and know His will. In 2020, Bella left her pushchair and walker behind when God told her through scriptures and prayer that she would not need them. About the same time God also healed her sister Naomi's vision.

Passing on the Faith, Lois and Eunice (Biblical Moms, Lois and Eunice)

For I am mindful of the sincere faith within you, which first dwelt in your grandmother Lois and your mother Eunice, and I am sure that it is in you as well. 2 TIMOTHY 1:5

Only one little sentence in the Bible mentions two women of faith. It reminds us that a mother and daughter's faith impacted the next generation. In his letter, Paul commends Timothy's mother and grandmother for passing on sincere and authentic faith to him. He sees them as authentic and living what they believe.

For mothers, our most important impact we can make is to live our faith and share it with the next generations. Faith will last when worldly things rust, brake, or pass away. These women raised this naturally shy child, Timothy, and Paul encouraged him to become bolder in sharing his faith.

Women of faith live a prayerful life, and their prayers would include God sending the right people into their children's lives. How wonderful for these women to see Paul take Timothy under his wing and love him like a son. Paul praised Timothy to the believers in Corinth and other churches so they might learn and be encouraged by this young man.

It's hard for mothers to let go and see a son move away and travel the world. But it's also a joy for mothers to see a son grow and become a great man who impacts many lives. They raised a missionary who served Paul and many believers. These two women poured their love and lived the example of faith. As we teach our little ones about God, read the Bible, and pray, we instill faith that can impact many lives. Lois and Eunice remind us that we are great influencers and that our faith can become a legacy.

What Can I Cook?

And who of you by being worried can add a single hour to his life?
MATTHEW 6:7

Rain poured for hours flooding the street and yard.

Becky shouted, "Mom we have a pond. Let's get ducks." Molly smiled as she recalled "duck" was her daughter's first word. She worried about her husband getting home.

The phone rang. Her husband planned to bring someone home for dinner. Molly hung up and said, "Daddy's bringing a man to dinner and I don't know what to cook. I don't know how they'll get home in the flood."

Becky said, "Daddy can take the ship home. He works on it. I'll make something in my kitchen." She looked at her plate of carrots and celery and added, "I can share my snack. It's healthy"

Molly laughed, "You're generous." She checked the refrigerator and freezer and said, "I can make shrimp and pea pods, some bread, and cookies."

"That sounds yummy, mommy. I can help cook."

Molly said, "I hope Dad's friend is not allergic to shrimp."

Becky said, "Let's pray that he likes it." What great thoughts come out of the mouth of babes! They prayed. Becky helped cook bread and cookies. Molly prayed until her husband and friend arrived. They sat for dinner, her husband blessed the food, and lifted the top off the covered dish.

Today's Mom Step

Listen to your children's faith when something seems impossible and pray with them.

The friend grinned and said, "I dreamed of shrimp and peapods all afternoon!"

Becky said, "We prayed you'd like shrimp and not be allergic to it." Everyone laughed. A childlike faith so easily trusts in God and encourages us as moms.

Fighting for Lives, Mildred Fay Jefferson (Historic Mom)

For God so loved the world, that He gave His only begotten Son, that whoever believes in Him shall not perish, but have eternal life. JOHN 3:16

As a girl, Millie followed the town doctor as he made house calls in his horse drawn buggy. The doctor answered her questions, and she told him she would become a doctor when she grew up. She grew up in Texas in the Jim Crow South, but that did not keep her from achieving great success, as indeed she did become a doctor.

Although motherless, Dr. Mildred Fay Jefferson fought for the life of unborn children. As a woman of faith and daughter of a minister, Mildred believed abortion violated the oath 'to do no harm." She fought against pre-abortion laws and declared that abortion made mothers enemies of defenseless babies with doctors becoming executioners.

Mildred made many firsts for African American women. She served as the first female surgeon general at Boston University Medical Center after being the first African American women to graduate from Harvard Medical School.

She served as the president of the National Right to Life Committee for three terms in the 1970s and wrote a column called "Lifelines" for their publication. As time went on, she became the most popular pro-life speaker in the U.S., stating, *"I became a physician in order to save lives, not to destroy them."* She pointed out that the nation's capital and other large cities had more black babies aborted than live births and referred to this tragedy as genocide.

> **Today's Mom Step**
>
> Look at your children and thank God for giving life to each one.

Mildred cared deeply about life that God creates. She saw each unborn baby as a living person who should be loved and treasured.

Faith with Run Away Rebels

Delight yourself in the LORD; And He will give you the desires of your heart. PSALM 37:4

Yvonne Ortega's son visited his dad and decided he wanted to stay. His father didn't set boundaries, a curfew, or many rules. He called his mom and said. "I'm staying with Dad. He's buying me a car." At sixteen, the car represented freedom and fun. Her ex had tried to use his money to influence their son and draw him away from her and her faith.

Yvonne felt her heart break but responded with love and said, "I'm here, and the door's open if you change your mind." She continued to pray daily that her ex would not be abusive and that her son would make the right choice. After suffering through years of abuse, Yvonne sought an end to the marriage when her husband started to abuse their son, so his decision to live with his father now scared her. She trusted God and prayed for protection for her son. She prayed he would listen to God's wisdom and not be drawn to material desires. She knew she needed to let go and trust her son to God.

A few weeks later her son called. He said, "I want to come home. Will you come and pick me up?"

Yvonne could not grab her keys fast enough and fought the urge to speed on the drive, all the while thanking God that the promised car was not enough. She praised God that her precious and only child chose her, their home, and the rules over lax parenting and a car. She was also thankful to God that she had the faith to stay firm about the rules and not try to go in debt competing with her ex to give her son things.

She hugged her son tightly and welcomed him home. She also reminded him her rules remained the same as did her unconditional love.

> **Today's Mom Step**
> Trust your children will learn from poor choices.

Week 20

Where Does a Mom Go to

Recharge?

Prayer for Energy

Dear Lord, thank you for my children and their energy and sense of adventure. Sometimes it seems as though they drain my energy faster than I can recharge. Please give me the energy I need to keep up with them.

Thanks for people in my life who also care for my children and give me needed breaks. It's refreshing to have time with girlfriends, a date with my husband, or time to shop. When I am exhausted, I pray you will be my strength. Restore my mind as well as my body so I can think straight. When little voices call my name whether day or night be with me and keep me calm and strong.

Help me to limit activities for my children and myself and manage my time that I might get the work in the home done and still enjoy the children. Let the hours I sleep be enough to refresh me.

When I am strong let me help my friends have a break so they can recharge.

Wisdom from Future Moms

Mom, I know how to go to sleep, so you'll be happy now. I just have to close my eyes.

I can make Mom smile by laughing.

Day Off

A generous person will prosper; whoever refreshes others will be refreshed. PROVERBS 11:25 (NIV)

Ginny phoned Melanie and said, "Surprise! I want you to have tomorrow off, so we'll take your children all day."

Melanie wasn't sure what to do with a day to herself. With her husband away at sea she had very little time alone, and much of her spare time was spent attending Bible study. She got a haircut and then went to the pool alone, relaxed, enjoyed the sunshine, and then wrote a letter to her husband. After that, she drove home and took a nap. Then she prepared and froze a few meals to have on days she felt exhausted, like recently when she woke up in the middle of the night to tend to one of her little ones. Later in the day she shopped and bought a gorgeous bouquet of fragrant flowers.

When Melanie drove up to pick up her three young children, Ginny opened the door and said, "Surprise! We have dinner ready for all of us." Wow! Dinner that included adults!

Melanie handed Ginny flowers and said, "You are so generous! Thank you for your kindness that refreshed me." Ginny gave Melanie a big hug. Melanie's children ran up and gave their mom a big hug."

Melanie's oldest child said, "Mommy, we had so much fun! We went in the pool, we played games, and we colored."

Her son grinned and showed her a picture he made.

> **Today's Mom Step**
>
> Help a friend take a needed break and thank anyone who gives you a break.

Melanie thanked Ginny's children for the fun activities they did with the children. Then the teens fed the little ones while

Melanie, Ginny, and Ginny's husband talked. Melanie expresses her thanks and said she felt so pampered and refreshed.

At Your (Biblical Mom, Peter's Mother-in-Law)

When Jesus came into Peter's home, He saw his mother-in-law lying sick in bed with a fever." MATTHEW 8:14

Jesus noticed this woman and saw her sickness. He healed her and she in turn waited on Jesus and her son-in-law Peter. This woman, Peter's mother-in law is not named but know only for her connection to a friend of Jesus. Jesus reached out to her and touched her hand without speaking a word. Their actions told the story.

The woman responded by getting up and serving her guests. This quiet woman did not run out and proclaim what Jesus did. Jesus did not question her about her faith or anything else. The simple act of service showed her faith and gratitude.

She kept her focus on Jesus and his friends whom she served. Neighbors and loved ones could wait to hear more later. She lived in the present and responded with a mother's love. Like any good Jewish mom, she served food. She never asked for healing but accepted the free gift of restored health.

We see no reaction from her son, Peter. He stood by as an observer. Peter had witnessed countless miracles, including Jesus healing a servant from a distance after listening to the plea of the servant's master. He brought Jesus to his home even with someone sick inside. Jewish customs would have prohibited Jesus from entering the home. Peter saw Jesus

> **Today's Mom Step**
> Serve the people around you with a grateful heart.

healing people everywhere, so having an ill woman in the house did not keep him from being hospitable.

It doesn't take a lot for Jesus to reach out to mothers-in-law. Jesus knows when our loved ones need help. He also knows each person's heart condition and faith. This woman responded by serving her son Peter and Jesus whom he followed.

Moms Night Out

And if one can overpower him who is alone, two can resist him. A cord of three strands is not quickly torn apart. ECCLESIASTES 4:12

Amy and Di emailed their girlfriends to schedule a night out. They met up at a local restaurant for half-price appetizers and time together. The table filled with dips, chicken wings, little clams, eggrolls, and more. They shared the food plus the ups and downs of the week. Whether they shared stories of someone's child's latest escapade or a new way of getting a child to clean a room they added in more ideas that got everyone laughing. They also commiserated with each one's problems like Cheri's mom's cancer or Elisa's husband's deployment. They offered support. Getting together and listening relieved stress.

They scheduled some other nights out that included crafting, bowling, walking on the beach, and a game night.

Amy said, "I heard about an escape room. We all get locked in a room for an hour and need to figure out how to escape. We find clues and solve puzzles. There's a theme with a story. How's that sound?"

Susie said, "Anytime I get away from an hour or so is an escape. I'm up for trying it."

The group enjoyed each activity and felt so recharged each time they gathered. They could talk for hours. Amy knew she'd be a sweeter and happier mom the coming week as she let go of stress. Di knew it was easier to accept her own kids being kids with them wanting to skip the schoolwork and cleaning since she her friends had the same struggles with their children. She considered trying to be less OCD about germs and cleaning the house. Being with friends made her realize she was a normal mom!

> **Today's Mom Step**
> Schedule a mom's night out that's affordable and fun for all your girlfriends.

Letters of Support, (Historic Mom, Abigail Adams)

By the river on its bank, on one side and on the other, will grow all kinds of trees for food. Their leaves will not wither and their fruit will not fail. They will bear every month because their water flows from the sanctuary, and their fruit will be for food and their leaves for healing. EZEKIEL 47:12

Abigail Adams's dedication as wife and mother showed through her many letters. She corresponded with her husband and her son, John Quincy, anytime they were apart. A few letters reveal that her husband John knew that tea refreshed her. Alas, one mix-up with tea he sent her ended up being delivered to his cousin Samuel Adams's wife, Elizabeth. John expressed his regret that she did not receive the gift, "I flattered myself that you would have the poor relief of a dish of good tea, under all your fatigues with the children, and all the disagreeable circumstances attending the small-pox." He quickly ordered a new box of tea to be sent to Abigail.

She and her husband reminded their children to practice virtue, study hard, and continue to learn, plus stressed the importance of history and philosophy. Abigail even took her son to a hill to watch the Battle of Bunker Hill to witness the cost of patriotism and freedom. There they watched Dr. Joseph Warren, a close family friend and the doctor who saved John Quincy's forefinger from amputation, die. Their tears mingled at that sight, and the memory remained with John all his life. He praised his mother and called her an angel upon earth and a blessing to all people within her sphere. She continued teaching John long into his adulthood through letters

Abigail also taught her son and other children the importance of scripture. John Quincy read the Bible in various languages and became a leader in the American Bible Society. Living through hard times of war and establishing a new nation, Abigail found comfort in correspondence and tea at home and with friends.

> **Today's Mom Step**
>
> Enjoy a cup of your favorite brew with a friend or write a letter to mail to her.

Friend Call

I urge Euodia and I urge Syntyche to live in harmony in the Lord. PHILIPPIANS 4:2

Mary and Kay were only neighbors for a few years, but the friendship lasted decades. From parenting to grandparenting, they still felt connected. They might have long lapses between talks, but it only took seconds to reconnect.

The two gals had been prayer partners, and their children played together when they were young. They liked each other on social media and checked out the other's posts. Every so often a post would be the inspiration for "I saw what you wrote and just had to call."

They shared the painful memories of divorce for the one and widowhood for the other. God's faithfulness through those times sustained them and became a witness for each other.

GROWING A MOTHER'S HEART

Kay said, "We've learned to live in harmony as Paul urged Euodia and Syntyche. *Euodia* means 'good journey' or 'success.' It makes me think about our struggles as journeys where God brings us through, and that's a success with lessons learned."

Mary replied, "*Syntyche* means 'happy event.' That's like a special blessing from God."

Kay said, "We've learned to be content in either circumstance. When it's a journey we always pray for the other and lend support. When it's a blessing we rejoice for the other without jealousy. We trust God in whatever is happening."

Mary said, "Yes. I am always so happy when you post good news, and [I'm] always praying for you."

"Same here and always will." Kay replied.

> **Today's Mom Step**
>
> Rejoice with a friend's happiness, be empathetic to her struggles, and trust God as you know you will both have your share of struggles and joys.

Week 21

Around the Table

Prayer for a Hospitable Spirit

Lord, let my home be a welcoming place where friends and family can sit, talk, eat, and play. Help me salt my conversation with grace. Guide me; grow my family with love, and bring our children up with faith in you.

May our meals be pleasant and filled with laughter and empathy for one another. May kindness start within my heart and home so my loved ones will want to return and bring their friends. Help me be a mom who nurtures my family, both body and soul.

Thank you for provisions of food you provide to feed all who come to the table. Help me make my home a place of beauty, peace, and safety. Help me be a mom whose children will feel free to talk about anything with me.

Help me discipline with love and yet provide the firmness my children need. Guide me in the home to grow my children into adults who make good choices in faith, work, and relationships.

May I also appreciate the hospitality friends extend to me and my family. Let us enjoy the company and time we come together.

Wisdom from Future Moms

Dad married mom cause she's a good cook and he likes to eat.

I know what moms do best: cook!

Joy's Family Coronavirus Dinners

Jesus then took the loaves, and having given thanks, He distributed to those who were seated; likewise also of the fish as much as they wanted. JOHN 6:11

When Joy realized their family needed to stay home for a pandemic, she wanted to make it fun for her family. She chose to have themed dinners and enlist members to take charge of some of the nights. They had to use supplies and food they had on hand. Her family loved to travel, so the teens quickly choose France, Italy, and even China. For places they had actually visited they chatted about their memories. For ones they'd like to visit, they shared facts and dreams.

They each set up a centerpiece display of the country and chose foods to make from that part of the world. Her daughter Emma made crepes for the dinner celebrating France, reflecting a meal she had enjoyed in Paris.

They also decided to have an experiment with fries and chicken nuggets to help local food places. They picked up fries from four places, and everyone, blindfolded, tasted a sample of each and attempted to identify the restaurant that made it. Their son Patrick cooked a variety of seafood one night, and they ate to the merry tunes from *The Little Mermaid* for a sea festival.

Today's Mom Step

Plan and hold a themed family dinner.

They also created meals to celebrate biblical accounts that included mutton (dressing as shepherds) and small bread loaves and fish (while reading about Jesus feeding the 5,000).

Another time they set up a picnic in the living room. They also set up some game nights, like Family Feud to play while eating. Laughter and building memories continued for weeks. Each family member kept their preparations secret to surprise the family.

Persistent Canaanite Mother
(Biblical Mom, Canaanite Mom)

But she said, "Yes, Lord; but even the dogs feed on the crumbs which fall from their masters' table." MATTHEW 15:27

One woman came to Jesus for help. She cried out for mercy for her daughter who needed healing.

Jesus ignored her until his disciples asked Him to send her away. He turned to the woman and said that He was sent to the lost sheep of the Israelites. The Canaanites had remained enemies of the Israelites since Old Testament times.

She walked closer, knelt next to Jesus, and again asked for help. This woman, not allowed to touch men or even make advances toward them, boldly came to Jesus.

Jesus replied that it's wrong to toss food to dogs that's meant for the children. This depicted the gentiles as dogs not fit to eat what God had for His people.

The words did not deter this mother. She believed Jesus could give her the help needed, so she replied that even dogs eat crumbs that fall from the owner's table. She didn't care if He called her a name or thought more of the people of Israel. She placed her hope in this man, the one she'd heard healed many people.

Jesus praised her great faith and said that her request was granted. He healed the daughter at that moment. Good mothers persist in finding the right help for their children. They set aside pride and focus on the need and where to get help. This mama

knew help comes from God. She did not care how many people heard her cries for help or listened to Jesus scold her. Jesus rewarded her faith and trust in Him.

Visitors and the Bread Plate

Jesus came and took the bread and gave it to them, and the fish likewise. JOHN 21:13

Rebecca and Darlene set the table. Another guest knocked on the door, and the girls added another setting. After everyone sat and Dad blessed the meal, they started passing the dishes of food. A guest took a biscuit and said, "What a colorful bread plate."

Darlene said, "We made it. It's our Jesus plate. Do you know Jesus is with us as we eat?"

The guest asked other questions, and various children chimed in to share more about the bread plate that had the words, "Loving from the Lord" on it. Their mom loved baking bread, and their family had made a few decorated bread plates.

The guest asked, "What happens if you don't have any bread?"

Rebecca replied, "Mom reminds us that we don't live on bread alone but on God's word, so we put scriptures on the plate and read them."

"Who made these warm fluffy biscuits?"

Rebecca said, "Mom made the biscuit batter yesterday. I took it out, rolled the dough, and cooked them. She added, "We've all helped mom make bread since we were babies when she'd give us a lump of bread to knead."

Darlene said, "Sometimes we put prayers on the bread plate or crackers. Even crackers are a type of food made with grain like bread."

Today's Mom Step
Serve bread and remind children that Jesus is the Bread of life.

Rebecca said, "Once in a while, we have an agape meal. That's just bread and grapes to remind us of communion."

The guest said, "You have a smart mom. I'll have to get a bread plate for my house."

A Faithful Mom's Influence
(Historic Mom, Morrow Graham)

Her children rise up and bless her; her husband also, and he praises her, saying "Many daughters have done nobly, but you excel them all." PROVERBS 31:28-29

Solidarity is a word Billy Graham used to speak about his mother. Morrow Graham made sure her family with their four children gathered together around at the table and with her and their father to listen to Bible stories and to pray. They also sat in front of the radio to listen to favorite shows and the latest news. Living on a dairy farm inherited from family and set amid gently rolling hills, they worked hard, but always took time to cultivate their faith.

Billy said his mother had the greatest influence on him of all the people he ever knew. That's something every mom would love to hear. Born in 1892, she had little education but spent time in devotions every day and could quote scriptures verbatim.

Many people called her Mother Graham. She taught music lessons, Sunday school, and sang in the church choir.

Billy's parents had a close relationship. When he attended Bible College, his parents prayed together every morning at ten. Billy observed that although they might sometimes storm at one another, they weathered the tempests. She greeted all guests with a friendly, "Come in come in, you are so welcome."

Morrow taught Billy to love books and reading. As a boy, he enjoyed adventure books like *Tom Swift* and *Robin Hood*. He also followed her example of working hard and seeing dignity in work. Morrow handled the bookkeeping for the farm, chopped wood for the stove, stitched needlepoint, and grew vegetables for the family. She taught Billy to garden, and the muscadine grapes he planted at the farm grew for decades.

> **Today's Mom Step**
> Pray daily for your children to be close to God.

Table Talk

Let no unwholesome word proceed from your mouth, but only such a word as is good for edification according to the need of the moment, so that it will give grace to those who hear. EPHESIANS 4:29

After Dad blessed the food, James sat with his food not touched. Mom asked, "What's on your mind James?"

He said, "I'm tired of doing the same old reports. I have to do one on the town library."

His brother said, "Well you're a bookworm, so maybe you can make a long bookworm and write on that." James laughed and shook his head.

Everyone asked questions: "How long does it need to be? What are the rules?"

GROWING A MOTHER'S HEART

James answered that he knew he could do a poster, but that seemed lame, and he needed at least fifteen facts. His sister suggested a 3D poster.

James replied, "Maybe I could make doors and windows that open like an advent calendar and write facts inside each piece that opens."

Mom replied, "That would be cool."

His brother laughed and said, "A peek-a-boo report! That sounds like fun to make."

They chatted about facts James knew and could ask librarians about, like how many books are in the library, and how many did they have when it opened. They also talked about what everyone did that day and shared some jokes.

Dad said, "This was a great meal. James, if you want, I'll take you to the store to buy poster board."

James nodded, and they headed out, and the others helped mom clean the table.

> **Today's Mom Step**
>
> At your family dinner talk about problems, the day's activities, and share stories or jokes.

Week 22

Community

Prayer for My Community

Lord, bless my hands and feet to serve others with your love. Give me the strength needed for what you call me to do. Help my hands to cook and bring a neighbor in need a meal or treat. Help me hear joy in children playing and yet also listen to needs when a neighbor faces various difficulties. Show me new ways to be kind to others daily.

Let me be thankful for smiles and acts of kindness I receive. Let me rejoice when new neighbors move in and greet them with a treat and offer to help. Let my heart rejoice at all the cultures that mix in the community and celebrate both our uniqueness and the similarities we share.

Making a community a happy place begins with one person. I am willing to be one person who can impact my neighbors. Bless my friends and all the people in my community and keep it safe.

Wisdom from Future Moms

God made moms because dads need help finding things.

Well, mom is right to punish me if I don't do my work, but I still don't like it. We both lose, because she still doesn't like that I didn't do my work.

Neighbors Helping Neighbors

"Which of these three do you think proved to be a neighbor to the man who fell into the robbers' hands?" And he said, "The one who showed mercy toward him." Then Jesus said to him, "Go and do the same." LUKE 10:36–37

Karen saw the wind damage inside her home. She saw broken windows, holes in roofs, and rubble strewn all over yards and driveways throughout the neighborhood. After the hurricane, the community looked like a war zone.

Frank from two houses down stopped by, knowing Karen's husband was off on military orders. He helped her teen son board up the front door. Her brother-in-law who lived an hour north, where the storm did not hit, called before her phone line died. He showed up later with tarps for the roof.

Someone Karen met at church just prior to the storm showed up and helped clear the driveway to be able to get the car out of the garage. Two of the men who worked for her husband showed up and helped her fix the fence. Her daughters thanked each with a loaf of homemade bread from the loaves they baked the day before the storm hit.

Later that week, after her husband returned, they held a block party in Karen's driveway to share food thawed due to three days without electricity. That helped everyone share needs and offer help. During the party the electricity came back on, and everyone cheered!

Karen called a friend with MS. They struggled with no power and found themselves constantly refueling the generator. Her friend and her

---

Today's Mom Step

Fill an emergency kit and add in extra supplies for neighbors.

---

daughters moved in while her husband remained at his house to work on clearing debris and doing repairs that he could do himself.

Karen took in laundry for other friends without power, and her family all helped wash and fold clothes. Friends stopped to take showers, pick up their laundry, chat, and share hugs.

Fresh Start Group (Biblical Moms, Joanna, Suzanna, Mary Magdalene)

Joanna the wife of Chuza, the manager of Herod's household; Susanna; and many others. These women were helping to support them out of their own means. LUKE 8:3

Joanna, Suzanna, and Mary Magdalene followed Jesus and supported Him. They may have given him money, washed clothes, and cooked meals. The women shared something else in common. Jesus had cured each of them from a disease of evil spirits. They found wholeness through Jesus.

Whether the women received forgiveness for a checkered past or healing from disease, the fresh start each received bonded them together. They came as friends to listen to Jesus and gave what they could to help him.

Imagine the joy the women shared with release from past pain. The excitement of the words Jesus shared and watching Him heal others would have reinforced their own healings. Freedom inspired generosity. Love received fills our hearts to pour out love generously to one another. These women may have sung as they traveled and become a lovely chorus of praise surrounding Jesus and the disciples.

Chuza and any other married woman probably returned in the late afternoon to prepare a meal and spend time with her family. The new sparkle of joy must have filled their homes with cheer. Hopefully that spilled over into the hearts of their spouses and children who may have rejoiced over her healing and felt new zest for life. These family members probably seemed different to people around them. Life witnesses of people led more people to follow Jesus until these groups became large crowds. Seeing change impacts people and build a more vibrant community.

Blessed by Community

Be kind to one another, tender-hearted, forgiving each other, just as God in Christ also has forgiven you. EPHESIANS 4:32

Camy loved her community. She enjoyed the parades and picnics the community planned and getting to know her neighbors. She invited some moms to bring their children over to make chocolates at her home. A few families came, and they made molded chocolates, dipped pretzels, and also dipped some fruit in the melted chocolates.

When holidays came, Camy invited the children again and asked them to bring friends. A mom or two offered to help. Camy covered a few tables with clear plastic to make cleanup easy and asked the older children who had made candy with her before to help teach those making chocolates for the first time. She showed them how to use edible paints to color the chocolates, and how to make some filled chocolates. Each time she taught a new skill.

One time her friend Amy came, and fourteen children showed up. In the middle of the fun the house began to shake, and Camy yelled, "It's an earthquake. Sit still." She stood in front of the only piece of furniture that could possibly topple. The tremor was not strong, so they did not have to run out. It lasted a few minutes.

Amy said, "Wow! Thank God we are safe. I know you've lived all over. Have you been in one before? You were so calm."

Camy replied, "Yes, in California. But it's so odd to have one on the east coast." They turned on the TV and watched news about the earthquake to

> **Today's Mom Step**
> Create fun for neighbors and their children to enjoy.

learn the epicenter was miles away across the bay, but for now it had stopped. They let the children go home with their goodies.

Gold Star Moms (Historic Mom)

Behold, a great wind came from across the wilderness and struck the four corners of the house, and it fell on the young people [all Job's children] *and they died, and I alone have escaped to tell you."*
JOB 1:19

A car drives up, soldiers in dress uniform steps out, one knocks at the door and then shares the sad news that a spouse has died in service to their country. They add, "We're sorry for your loss."

Since WWI, women have banded together to support one another when they have family members serving. Those with children serving are called Blue Star Mothers. During war times, many hang a star in the window for each member serving. They rally around when one receives devastating news that a friend has become a Gold Star mom. Each knows, "It could have been me."

During WWII, when Alleta's husband answered the door and asked, "Which one?" the response, "All five" brought the worst news possible. A torpedo sunk the ship where they all served together. A follow up letter from the Navy ended with the words, "I know you will carry on in the fine Navy Spirit." The three remaining Sullivans did that. Their daughter served in the WAVES. Alleta and her husband traveled the country, speaking and urging factory workers to maximize production. They knew many others lost sons and loved ones for the cause of freedom.

Blue Star moms send care packages, collecting donations for children of military serving abroad, making albums for Gold Star moms, visit wounded soldiers if any receive treatment near them, and encourage one another. The Gold Star club is not one they want to join, but they trust the support will be real and ready if that day comes. For pregnant moms, they give baby showers and stay with them during the pregnancy and beyond. For all, they offer hugs and support.

> **Today's Mom Step**
>
> When someone in your circle of friends receives bad news, be ready to help in a number of ways, including caring for children, fixing meals, and sometimes, just simply listening.

Recharged by Community

So that I may come to you in joy by the will of God and find refreshing rest in your company. ROMANS 15:32

PeggySue Wells enjoyed meeting up with the mom's playgroup at the local park each Friday. She homeschooled, and this gave everyone a break. The children all needed to have the week's work caught up, or they all stayed home. One challenging week, PeggySue noticed that the children seemed restless and grumpy as they argued and picked on one another. In her mind, she kept complaining too. They needed a break. She said, "Let's go to the park, although work is unfinished. I think we all need a break. Just promise to catch up later."

The children applauded and raced for the van. PeggySue sat at a picnic table and joined the conversation as the women all shared their good and bad days from the week. They vented, laughed, shared tips, and encouraged one another. As she said goodbye she added, "I feel so refreshed. We almost stayed home to catch up, but I need this more than the extra time for work. It's the best medicine for this mom!"

She had watched her little gang of seven as they laughed and played. Heading home in the van she asked what each child did. She listened as each one shared about the fun they enjoyed. She listened harder. No grumps and no complaints from anyone. PeggySue asked, "Anyone think they have enough energy to finish up the week's work when we get home. Everyone agreed they could tackle it. She said, "The park recharged us. I've decided this time is special. Park time with our friends is our refreshment and recharging time that will not have any rules attached on whether all our work is done or not." The children cheered.

> **Today's Mom Step**
> Identify what refreshes you and your children and make sure to schedule those activities.

Week 23

Balancing Act

and Simpler Life

Prayer for Balance

Dear Lord, my days are so busy like most of the moms around me. Help me choose wisely how to spend my time. I want to invest in my family and not only focus on housekeeping and discipline. I want to make sure there's time every week for each family member and time for self-care. When my calendar looks simple with days balanced, I am so much happier and calmer.

I also want to do what you call me to do. I know there is a season to everything, and sometimes the call is to prepare now and jump in later. Let me have the strength to face each day's challenges and to rejoice at the blessings and wonders of motherhood. Help me to not crowd my days with what is not necessary, but to fill it with what is meaningful. Let me be a living example of a Christian mom to draw others to follow you.

Wisdom from Future Moms

If I do my work, mom gives me a reward. It's usually five cents, a candy, or playing with a cool stuffed animal. It's worth it especially the five cents.

Moms do so many different things. They are multitaskers.

Garbage Truck Race

The earth was formless and void, and darkness was over the surface of the deep, and the Spirit of God was hovering over the surface of the waters. GENESIS 1:2 (NKJV)

Alice answered the phone and panicked. "What do you mean this Saturday? I thought it was the following week?" Ugh! She overbooked herself again. A thirty-minute drive separated the places she needed to be Saturday. The leader rescheduled her to later in the day. She heard the garbage truck and panicked again. Her oldest son took all the garbage out with no reminder. Did he take out silver garbage bags that held craft supplies? She raced outside. No bags. She ran inside. The bags stored for months and taken out of the attic the night before no longer sat on the floor. She called the dump. They checked and said the truck was just heading back to the dump.

She donned her coat, tossed a scarf over her face and hat on her head to hide her face and dressed her three-year-old in warm clothes. She arrived before the truck, and the workers told her where to stand, quizzing her about the lost items, "a diamond, wallet, keys, heirloom?"

Alice replied, "No, but it's important. She looked at the pine trees surrounding the dump and told her daughter to remain in the van. The truck drove in and they slowly unloaded it as she searched. No silver bags! One man said, "Don't give up. A few get stuck in the top. Yes, he pulled out two silver bags. She grabbed them, yelled thanks, and thought, "I'll never tell a soul."

The men laughed and pointed, "You did this for pinecones?" She nodded. They were huge ones perfect for children to decorate as gifts for Christmas. Alas, her daughter told everyone about their adventure. Alice prayed for better time skills. God pointed her to the creation chapter of Genesis 1, which emphasizes the

Today's Mom Step

Balance time with a good calendar or system and God's example from chaos to creation.

importance of managing one task at a time, sorting things, and focusing on fruitful choices. That made life better!

Hello, Mom (Biblical Mom, Mother of the Sons of Thunder)

Then the mother of the sons of Zebedee came to Jesus with her sons, bowing down and making a request of Him. MATTHEW 20:20

One helicopter mom in the Bible wanted the best for her two sons. That's what most moms want. Her sons must have shared what they did with her. Two days before she approached Jesus, He told His disciples, His close friends, about their reward in heaven. He said, "You who have followed Me, in the regeneration when the Son of Man will sit on His glorious throne, you also shall sit upon twelve thrones, judging the twelve tribes of Israel" (Matthew 19:28).

What a great promise, but somehow this mama wanted more. She asked Jesus to let her sons sit closest to him, one on His left side and one on His right side. She dared to try and manipulate Jesus, God the Son. He did not fall for her request. He explained that God the Father made those decisions, and they came at a price she could not grasp. He said she did not understand her own request as she did not know what it would mean to drink the cup He had to drink. Like many helicopter moms who want preference for their children, she stirred up lots of emotions. The other disciples felt offended, and Jesus had to calm everyone down.

Jesus shared a secret that's good for moms to know. He said that those who want to be great must be servants. Moms, instead of pushing for the best for your children and making them feel privileged and spoiled, be grateful for their blessings and help them learn to care about others and serve others. This gets them noticed more in a good way without stirring up jealousy or anger. Love your children enough to encourage them to love others.

Today's Mom Step

Encourage your children to be kind and help other people; to spy out needs and fill them.

Jesus asks us to follow His example. He came to serve, and He is our example.

What's the Best Choice for My Kids?

Give thanks to the LORD with the lyre; Sing praises to Him with a harp of ten strings. PSALM 33:2

PeggySue Wells had limited funds, as many young people do, so she carefully considered and prayed about choices for extracurricular activities that would keep money balanced. She said, "I chose music because no matter how old the children became, or what physical condition they may be in, they pretty much could do music."

That choice equipped her seven children to teach music to pay their way through college and to continue to make money as stay-at-home parents. They enjoyed music as siblings all their lives together. Genres, instruments, composers, and creativity had no limits, so they could explore in the field. As extra opportunities and funds allowed, they added sports, and horseback riding. Music remained their flagship, and Peggy Sue found the right teacher for each unique child.

For example, her daughter Leilani learned differently, more like exuberant Anne of Green Gables and saw beauty that inspired her everywhere. PeggySue called the only piano teacher in town only to discover the waiting list stretched a few years. A few days later, the teacher called back and said, "I've prayed about your daughter and think I should squeeze her in for half an hour a week."

Leilani took to the music quickly. One day she asked, "Mommy was Bach a nice man?"

Her mother replied that she thought so since he composed music for his wife.

Leilani replied, "Good. Then he won't mind my fixing his music." Her teacher applauded the little girl's original rendition and then asked her to play the score the way Bach composed it. That helped her appreciate the master and understand the difference between the compositions.

Mother at the Rock
(Historic Mom, Mary Ball Washington)

You shall teach them [God's Word] *diligently to your sons and shall talk of them when you sit in your house and when you walk by the way and when you lie down and when you rise up.* DEUTERONOMY 6:7

George Washington led one of the greatest victories against the worst odds to bring freedom to America. He made advances in agriculture as a farmer, and his home become a place open to countless visitors. He helped forge this nation and set it up with elected leaders that replaced a monarchy. What did the mother of the first President of the United States do to raise such a successful son?

Mary focused on prayer and stretching money to provide all she could. George's father died when George was eleven, and on his deathbed, he gave George three books on prayer. Mary never remarried but managed the family estates until her George grew old enough to take over.

Mary often went to "Prayer Rocks" in Fredericksburg to read, pray, and meditate. Later in her life, George purchased a home for her four blocks from that spot. Many historians have called her controlling and stern while family members remarked on her kindness. This strong and resilient single mother, orphaned at age thirteen, raised her sons to be responsible and hard workers with ordered lives. She lived in a time that few women could survive well without a husband. Her sons all served in the military. As a teen she read devotional books and developed a strong religious conviction. She raised George to be a gentleman, schooling him in social settings such as having tea (that she loved drinking) with others, and providing dancing lessons for him.

George wrote, "All that I am I owe to my mother. I attribute all my success in life to the moral, intellectual, and physical education I received from her." She molded George's character with Bible reading and the *Contemplations Moral and Divine* by Sir Matthew Hale. One nephew depicted her as someone he feared yet called her a kind person.

Today's Mom Step

Read the Bible with your children.

Sew Sensible

She senses that her gain is good; Her lamp does not go out at night.
PROVERBS 31:18

Marion stayed up to finish her sewing. She worked during the day while she homeschooled the children. New customers came to her weekly as people showed off their clothes she made. She could pause and check assignments, listen to children read, and earn some money to add to her husband's income. This helped pay for extras like sports, dance lessons, and books.

Then moms started asking to take sewing lessons. She set up a class and had her children clear desks once a week in the morning and used that time for them to do art and music. Moms carried in their machines, and she taught them. Then they wanted their children to learn to sew.

Marion chose to first train each child in the care and use of the machine. She created a sewing license to earn before sewing any garments or stuffed animals. Each child needed to practice threading, sewing straight lines on paper, and then curved lines. They learned to cut fabric, stitch by hand, and use a seam ripper. With each class she allowed one of her own to participate and learn to sew. The children progressed and made simple curtains for their rooms, stuffed animals, and t-shirts. She paid her children who helped prepare and clean up from the classes she taught.

One of her daughters decided to start a small business of making and selling stuffed animals. Marion enjoyed watching some of her students put their talent to use in making costumes for the home school group's performances and staging fashion shows. The moms applauded her sensible sewing classes

> **Today's Mom Step**
> Use your talents to earn a little extra cash and equip your children with life skills.

that equipped the children and moms with life skills and her ability to balance it with her own home schooling.

Week 24

A Listening Heart

Prayer for a Listening Heart

Lord, give me a listening heart and wisdom as my children talk. I am easily distracted and want to really listen to what's in their hearts behind the words. I want to understand the real needs and respond with love.

Let me give my whole attention to my family as we talk, look into their eyes, and really empathize with each one. We all need to be heard, and I am thankful you always listen to me. When I hear the hurt in my child's voice, let me listen with love. Where I hear excitement and rejoicing, let me applaud and rejoice also.

Let me also listen to my friends, supports, and people I encounter, that I might have an understanding heart. Help me respond with encouragement.

I want my children to know I will always listen, even if I do not always agree. I want us to know we can love even when we are not in harmony on some choices. Let my heart be ready to forgive and be willing to change as you guide me.

As we grow as a family in the Lord, help us listen to the needs of friends and people around us. Help us to respond when we listen.

Wisdom from Future Moms

Mom gets mad and says I should do my chores, or I won't know how to do those skills when I grow up.

I know your mom listens to me when she looks me in the eye.

Mom, Listen to What I Want!

He who gives an answer before he hears, it is folly and shame to him. PROVERBS 18:13

Stef wanted a TV in her room. They kept the TV in the family room so everyone could watch together, so Becky Harling wasn't a fan of Stef's new idea. Stef had reasons a-plenty for why she wanted this. Becky whispered a prayer for wisdom. Thankfully, God gave her an idea. Becky told Stef to go to the office and write a proposal on the computer for why she needed a TV in her room. She told her to use good sentence structure and well-formed paragraphs. She reminded her to use spell check and advised her that it would have to be grammatically correct.

Stef's eyes lit up, and she enthusiastically took on the challenge. Several hours later, Stef handed her a well-written proposal. As soon as Stef left the room for Steve and Becky to discuss and reach a decision about her proposal, they looked at each other in shock. They had the same reaction, "Wow! This is good! Now what are we going to do?" Honestly, Becky hadn't expected Stef to work so hard on it. Stef had worked for hours, and now they had a decision to make.

After a few moments of debate, Steve said, "You know, Beck, I think Stef needs a win! We have to say no quite a bit. I think she needs a win on this one." Then Steve reminded her that they had an old black-and-white TV in the garage that only worked on about three channels. Steve said, "Why don't we give her that one?"

Stef was thrilled! Her parent's decision affirmed her

Today's Mom Step

Listen to your child's needs and for difficult ones ask them to write a proposal.

---

proposal and ability to articulate what she wanted and why she had that desire. Again, the Spirit of God reminded Becky that He had given Stef a strong voice to use for His glory. She actually only watched TV twice in her room. The color TV in the family room with more channels was a much greater draw.

Diplomatic Mom (Biblical Mom, Priscilla)

He [Apollos, a new convert] *began to speak out boldly in the synagogue. But when Priscilla and Aquila heard him, they took him aside and explained to him the way of God more accurately.* ACTS *18:26*

Priscilla and her husband served in an early church in Corinth. The Apostle Paul shared the same business career of making tents, so Paul stayed in their home on his missionary journey. He trained them. They later listened to an eloquent speaker named Apollos, a new convert who was fired up on speaking about Jesus but not as knowledgeable. He got some things wrong.

Priscilla and Aquila took Apollos aside to explain God's ways more accurately. With gracious understanding, they did not embarrass him, but quietly guided him. They became spiritual parents and mentors to this man. Apollos took the instruction well as seen in what he did next. He chose to go to Achaia to preach, and Priscilla and the other Christians prayed for him and wrote letters to people they knew in the area he would travel to, recommending him. He was powerful in his speech and did much to help the people he ministered to, demonstrating real truths about Jesus.

Spiritual moms are important, and we hope to also be those types of mentors to our own children as well as to new Christians and friends. Listening first to what Apollos shared helped

Priscilla approach him. She could praise him for his enthusiasm and his working on being accurate. Then she and Aquila could also share more truths to enlighten him. They did not correct him in public but avoided embarrassing him with a private discussion. The private chat showed their respect and love, which built the relationship and made them the perfect couple to recommend him and rejoice at his new successes.

An Apple Lesson

This you know, my beloved brethren. But everyone must be quick to hear, slow to speak and slow to anger. JAMES 1:19

"I'm so full, but what I really want is an apple." Mom said.

Sean got up, went to the bowl, grabbed a bright red apple, returned, and handed it to his mom with a big smile.

Mom stared at the apple until Dad said, "You said you really wanted an apple."

Mom laughed. She meant to say napkin but happened to look at a bowl of bright red apples and used the wrong word. She said, "Thanks for listening. I did not pay attention to my own words. I wanted a napkin but happened to look at the beautiful apples."

Her son went and got her a napkin. She thanked him for being such a good listener.

The phrase "What you really want is an apple," became a family joke when someone didn't listen well or pay attention. Mom and Dad also shared a story from when they were first married, and company stayed with them. Mom placed plastic wrap in the fridge. When Dad questioned that she replied, "Because that's where I keep it."

The next day Mom asked her visitor if she had seen the plastic wrap. She replied, "Yes. In the fridge. Your husband said that's where you keep it. I wondered about your reason for that. Is it a special tip for cooking or storing leftovers?"

Mom raced over to the drawer that held usually held plastic wrap to see if she put leftovers there. Thankfully she had not. She laughed and said she must have been too tired to notice what she did or to really listen to her husband. She apologized to her husband and worked on listening better. She discovered listening is key to growing relationships.

> **Today's Mom Step**
>
> Actively listen when someone speaks and make sure you hear what is communicated.

Amelia Taylor, A Mom Who Listened (Historic Mom)

Make your ear attentive to wisdom, Incline your heart to understanding. PROVERBS 2:2

Amelia prayed her children would work to understand each other. She and her husband James taught the children and led them in worship through reading the Bible, praying, and singing. They welcomed many strangers into their home, and Amelia taught Bible classes for girls at church.

Young Hudson enjoyed spiritual studies and showed an interest in missionary work. At age fifteen he started working in a bank and followed the example of coworkers in swearing and mocking the Christian faith. He liked money and pleasure and started rebelling at home.

Amelia chose to respond with kindness and showed great patience with Hudson. She prayed even more for him. On a vacation, she pleaded with God until she believed God answered her prayer. Then she started praising God.

At home, Hudson felt bored and unhappy. He wandered around his home and picked up a tract called, "Poor Richard." He read the story and became convicted about Jesus and salvation. He knelt and committed his life to Christ. When mother and son reunited, Hudson said, "I have some news to tell you."

Amelia replied before he spoke any more words, "I know what it is. You have given yourself to God."

Today's Mom Step

Communicate with kindness and patience with your children especially when they make poor choices.

Hudson trained as a doctor and then left to be a missionary in China where he founded the China Inland Mission and ministered for fifty-one years. Mom and son communicated by letters, and Hudson relied on his mother's wisdom. He also learned that his parents dedicated him at birth to the Lord and to missionary work in China.

Walking, Listening, and Talking

Give me now wisdom and knowledge, that I may go out and come in before this people, for who can rule this great people of Yours?"
2 CHRONICLES 1:10

After a truck slammed into the van when sixteen-year-old Darla stopped at a red light, she suffered headaches and some memory loss. She had some PTSD. That made some of her schoolwork difficult, especially history and getting the timelines and facts straight. As a kinesthetic learner, Darla processed information better when she was physically active. She enjoyed walking, so she and her mom started taking evening walks to sum up learning from history class.

Darla liked to move as she learned, so this worked well. After "history walks," they simply talked, and her mom listened as Darla chatted about life, how she wanted healing, and about her future. Her mom mostly listened, especially to the dreams of her daughter's heart.

Darla also commented on her mom's parenting. One time she said, "Mom, I think you can be narrow-minded and opinionated about sex and other topics."

Her mom said, "There are times I need to know what's happening in the world and how culture changes, but when it is something to do with God's truth and principles, those are convictions. They are core beliefs that never change just because many people choose to turn away from God. I am willing to defend and die for Jesus as a follower of His truths."

Darla replied, "That is different. I would stay with Jesus on salvation and things. I want to think about what that means about other choices I make."

Her mom said, "It's always good to talk things over with God." She just listened over the next few weeks as Darla shared what she studied and believed. At times she would

> **Today's Mom Step**
>
> Be sure to study the Bible and know your core beliefs so you can share those with your children.

mention a Bible passage to add to her daughter's studies and would also respond to Darla's questions.

Week 25

Where's Your Sparkle?

Prayer for Restored Joy

Dear Lord, sometimes I am in the doldrums and weary. Help me get my sparkle on and fill my heart with joy. Refresh my spirit. Help me to model joy even when I struggle. Let me greet my family with joy each morning and send them off to bed with cheer.

On days of less energy, may I be filled with peace and contentment that share its own luster. Give me the energy I need each day. I want my children to rejoice and praise you with joy. Help me pass on joy to them. Let us find delight each day in blessings, in the world around us, and in the people we love. Let our blessings ignite joy. May our struggles bring us to pray and trust in you with the joyful expectation that you will respond. Let me choose joy!

Help my joy spill over to friends and family that they will also find joy in You.

Wisdom from Future Moms

Mommy, when are you going to go and put the blonde back in your hair? This other gray stuff makes you look kind of old.

Mom lost her sparkle, so I make her a big ole' tray of cookies.

Time to give you a foot massage mama. Close your eyes and relax.

Glitter Powder

There he was transfigured before them. His face shone like the sun, and his garments became as white as the light. MATTHEW 17:2

Emlee ran up with her mom to her neighbor, Mrs. Kay, and said, "I need some of your glitter powder. Mom is not sparkly today." Emlee had enjoyed a birthday party for Mrs. Kay's granddaughter, where she had dusted the girls with glitter powder for pixie dust.

They went in with Mrs. Kay and stayed for tea. Emlee's mom sat and had tea and closed her eyes to rest. Mrs. Kay got her powder and said, "Emlee, we can make some sparkle powder for you to take home. They mixed together one cup of tapioca starch, fifteen drops of vanilla oil, one ounce of clay powder called kaolin, and then Emlee sprinkled in some gold cosmetic glitter. She used a cotton ball to sprinkle some on her mom.

Mrs. Kay asked, "Emlee, how did your mom lose her sparkle?"

Emlee said, "Well, my brothers and friends and I played at our house and made a huge mess. Mom said we zapped all her energy, and I noticed she lost her sparkle."

Mrs. Kay asked, "Now you added sparkle outside. So, what are you doing to help her sparkle on the inside?"

Emlee said, "I think I better go home and clean. We left my brothers there to clean up too. If friends come, they will also have to clean." She turned, grabbed her mom's hand, and said," Mom. I'm ready to clean. You can take a nap on the couch."

Today's Mom Step

Let your children know if you lose your sparkle and let them help you get sparkly again.

Emlee's mom smiled. Later that day Mrs. Kay saw them, Emlee's mom, Emlee, and her brothers laughing and playing outside. Emlee shouted. "Mom has her sparkle everywhere again!"

Sparkle of Christ (Biblical Woman, Mary Magdalene)

But Mary was standing outside the tomb weeping; and so, as she wept, she stooped and looked into the tomb. JOHN 20:11

Mary didn't think she could feel worse, but when she saw the empty tomb, she wept. Jesus had been crucified and buried. She stood outside the tomb where His body had disappeared.

Two angels spoke to her and asked, "Woman, why are you weeping?" She replied that she didn't know what happened to the body of her Lord. She turned around, and Jesus stood there and asked the same question, "Woman why are you weeping?" She continued to have no sparkle, no joy, and asked where he had laid the Lord's body.

Then Jesus spoke her name, "Mary!" She finally realized Jesus stood there, alive! She left rejoicing and shared the good news. She announced, "I have seen the Lord!" Good news changes everything. That Jesus knows our names and calls out to us also changes us.

It's natural to grieve the loss of a loved one and hard to regain our sparkle at such times. Grief takes time to process. There are moments we feel we have no more tears left to shed, and yet they come again. Mary grieved a few long days and nights, and then thought she hit another low point—when Jesus met her and restored her joy. The resurrection of Jesus gives us all hope that when we lose a loved one, it is not the end. Jesus promises eternal life to all believers, and that gives reason for gratitude in the face of loss.

We will have periods when we mourn and times when we feel helpless or sad. Those are times to trust that the Lord will restore our sparkle and give us new reasons to be thankful and rejoice. Trust the Lord to restore your heart in His timing.

Mom Lost Her Sparkle

I have no greater joy than this, to hear of my children walking in the truth. 3 JOHN 4

Julia and her sisters knew what to do. Her mom didn't smile that morning. She lost her sparkle. Julia knew how to get it back. Her sisters and she started cleaning the house. One folded the mountain of clothes. One picked up trash and swept the floor. Another cleaned up the kitchen. They all put their clothes away.

After cleaning the house, they cut fruit to make a snack for when mom returned. They cut hearts and wrote reasons they love their mom and then stuck them on the front door. Each wrote a note to mom, telling her how they loved her. They even made her a crown with glittery chenille stems. Then they prayed together and asked God to help their mom get her sparkle back and to help them do a better job with their chores.

When mom came home, she smiled at the notes on the door. She walked inside, and the girls ran to hug her. She looked around and said, "You have cleaned up. The laundry piles all disappeared. Are you magicians?" They laughed and told her to have a seat. They brought her fruit and a cold drink. Julia brought in the crown, placed it on her head and said, "You are God's princess."

They handed her their notes. She ate, read, and thanked them. She said, "Girls, you made my week!"

> **Today's Mom Step**
>
> Be thankful when your children help you regain your sparkle.

Her daughter Julia said, "You lost your sparkle, and we wanted to help you get it back. We love you."

"I feel so sparkly now, from my head to my toes!" Mom said.

A Praying Mom, Susanna Wesley (Historic Mom)

The LORD said to Satan, "The LORD rebuke you, Satan! Indeed, the LORD who has chosen Jerusalem rebuke you! Is this not a brand plucked from the fire?" ZECHARIAH 3:2

Susanna Wesley lived a hard life with working and stretching the little money they had. The people at the church her husband pastored disliked him, so they didn't pay him well. He spent his time studying and writing about the sufferings of Job. Her children learned how she regained her sparkle on tough days. If they saw her lift her apron from the front of her skirt and toss it over her head to form a tent, they knew she was praying. When she let the apron down, they saw her renewed sparkle. She loved to pray and talk to God. She called it her tent of meeting.

She gave birth to nineteen children, but only ten lived. One of her children was crippled, and another had difficulty learning to walk. Susanna watched fires destroy two of their homes and burn all their possessions. She and her husband argued incessantly, but her prayers impressed her children—especially Charles and John. They grew up to preach and bring millions of people to know the Lord. They each had a sparkle in their voices.

As soon as each child spoke, Susanna taught that babe to recite the Lord's prayer. She homeschooled her children, and they all read by age five. She kept a schedule for meals, bedtimes, school, and naps and accompanied discipline with forgiveness. With her routines, the house remained quiet but busy. Susanna was a gifted speaker and taught the Bible, and up to two hundred women attended her teaching sessions.

> ### Today's Mom Step
> As needed, set up new routines to replace old ones to create order in the home.

John referred to himself as a brand plucked out of a fire because he almost died when one house burned down. A farmer saw him in a window amid leaping, glowing flames. Men climbed on top of each other to rescue John. His mother's prayers sparked his faith.

Transitions and Regaining Sparkle

So that they [older women] *may encourage the young women to love their husbands, to love their children. Titus 2:4*

Cynthia Simmons felt sad. Her youngest of four children entered a new phase by ending an old one. He stopped nursing. She knew that ended her time of nursing babies. Each time Caleb reached a new milestone, she felt a little sad, knowing it ended another phase of her days as a mom.

Cynthia thought, "When I stopped nursing Caleb, I grieved in my dreams, because I knew he was my last child. I loved the baby stage." She felt a similar sentiment when her youngest graduated from home school and thought, "I was finished homeschooling. A huge chunk of my life ended." She prayed for wisdom about what she should do in the next phase of parenting, especially as her children entered adulthood.

Cynthia chatted with younger moms and shared her wisdom. As she did that, she regained her sparkle and rejoiced in the stages they enjoyed at the time. She reset her thinking too and realized as one stage ended, a new adventure began.

Cynthia started writing and developed a podcast for mothers. She spoke to groups of homeschool moms. She became a mom encourager. Each encounter brought back wonderful memories that gave her joy. She listened to the moms and rejoiced in their experiences. As her children grew, she also realized she might one day have grandbabies to enjoy and nurture through the years. Each transition also gave her the opportunity of blessing others from her own experience.

> **Today's Mom Step**
> Enjoy your current stage of motherhood and trust the next one will have new adventures and joys.

Week 26

Words of Encouragement

Encouragement Prayer

Lord, help me use words to encourage my children. Let me cheer on their good choices, connect them to opportunities to use their gifts and talents, and inspire them to follow their calling.

Help me avoid nagging, scolding, and putting them down or using phrases that deflate their spirits.

Let me think before I speak so I can connect to each one's individual needs and abilities. Help me show appreciation when they assist me and praise them when they work hard and reach goals.

Help me give encouragement to other moms and people around me. Let me be a blessing to others with my words and prayers. Let me also encourage myself when I feel I have failed and remember the encouraging words you give me in scriptures.

Help me avoid words that would limit people or make them feel inadequate. Help me use words that show I am pleased with their efforts and I believe they can follow their dreams.

Wisdom from Future Moms

The best thing my mom does is play games with me, even though she loses most of the time.

I wish mom had more imagination. She chose names that begin with "D" for all of us, even daddy. Now she mixes up our names all the time except the dog. We named her Puffy.

Encouragement Eggs!

Or if he [a father] *is asked for an egg, he will not give him* [his son] *a scorpion, will he?* LUKE 11:12

Marsha and Val came around the corner on their morning walk to the surprise yells of a group of friends.

"Happy Birthday Marsha!"

Marsha started laughing and said, "I've been flash mobbed!"

Her daughter came up and handed her a gift bag. She opened it and found a pink plastic egg. Inside the egg she saw slips of paper. Each had a good word, sticker, or little picture."

Marsha hugged her daughter and said, "Wow! You gave me a good egg of encouragement.

Everyone rushed up and gave her eggs. Her husband handed her a golden egg. And asked her to open it right away. Inside that one he had written a poem, and one slip of paper said, "Dinner out, Molly's coming to babysit."

"Wow! This is a great day. I needed all this encouragement. Since I started back to school, I felt so slow and rusty."

Marsha's daughter said, "You give us a good egg when we do something great or when we are sad and need happy words, so I said we should all give you good eggs."

Val said, "Your daughter had me take her to our neighbors, where she gave each one an egg to fill with encouragement for you and told them her plan. Your husband sent the flash mob note out on social media."

Today's Mom Step

Give out a note or egg with words to encourage s friend or child. Keep a spare one in your purse for when you see someone who is sad.

Mary's Words (Biblical Mom, Mary)

His [Jesus's] *mother* [Mary] *said to the servants, "Whatever He says to you, do it."* JOHN 2:5

Mary overheard the waiters discuss a problem about a shortage of wine for the guests. When they finished pouring all the wine, Mary said to Jesus, "They have no wine."

He responded with a question. He asked how the lack of wine concerned him and stated that His time had not begun. Reading His words reminds us of the future banquet of Jesus as King, the Last Supper, and His shedding blood at His death. Mary proceeded with her desire that He help. Mary told the waiters, "Do whatever He says."

Jesus performed a miracle. He turned water in several large clay jugs into wine. Mary showed trust in Christ's ability to solve a problem that mere mortals could not solve. This humble woman who simply said 'yes' to God, quietly received shepherds and magi, and pondered words from Simeon and Anna at the temple, appears to be stronger willed here.

The words to the servants within the hearing of Jesus showed her trust and encouragement to help friends. She knew her son's heart. We see little of the childhood of Jesus, but we know He obeyed His parents (Luke 2:51). Here she showed total confidence in her son and His ability. She showed support for His ministry to people and opened a door for Jesus to reveal Himself as the Messiah. It reflects giving her son a blessing on His future work. We see a son entering adulthood who is starting to move away from child-

Today's Mom Step

Observe your child's bent, show confidence in good choices, and bless their ministry choices.

hood obedience to be a leader and follow the will of God the Father. As mothers we can impact our children for good when we show confidence in them and encourage them.

Encouraged to Speak

Then Moses said to the Lord, "Please, Lord, I have never been eloquent, neither recently nor in time past, nor since You have spoken to Your servant; for I am slow of speech and low of tongue." EXODUS 4:10

Bruce said, "Mom, my teacher wants me to take part in the Sunday School play. I don't want to do it."

"Do you want to be brave?"

"Yes, if God parted the sea like He did for Moses, I would lead everyone across."

"Moses did that. He also told God he was afraid to speak and spoke too slow. Do you know one of the biggest fears people have, even grownups?

He asked, "Being in a play?"

"Almost. It's speaking in front of people. That can be a play or just having to talk. God sent a helper to Moses, but then Moses also started talking to a humongous crowd."

"Everyone will look at me."

"You could hold a prop. That's an object or sign. Then they will look at what you hold."

"I want to be brave. I don't want God to think I would not lead people if He asks me. What will be my prop? Can I hold my hamster?"

"No, he will stay home. He could jump down, run around, and scare people."

"I'm supposed to be Noah. I could hold stuffed animals."

"That could work. Or some animal food. We need to talk to your teacher."

The night of the play, Bruce stood up straight and said all his lines with a monkey puppet around his neck. He waved the monkey's arm and let the monkey play peek-a-boo.

Today's Mom Step

Encourage your child be brave including with speaking.

Mom's Prayer for God's Call, Eliza Spurgeon (Historic Mom)

But Jesus said, "Let the children alone, and do not hinder them from coming to Me; for the kingdom of heaven belongs to such as these." MATTHEW 19:14

Praying with each child, Eliza prayed that each one might live before God. Her son John Archer Spurgeon wrote, "She was the starting point of all the greatness any of us, by the grace of God, have ever enjoyed."

Saturday evenings, the family sat around the table while Eliza read and explained the scriptures verse by verse. She also worked at helping each child read and apply the scriptures to build character. Alas, only eight of her seventeen children survived infancy.

Eliza supported her husband's ministry. Since he traveled often to preach, she kept the home and taught their children. She spent extra time praying for their son due to his strong-will. When her son began preaching and moved away, she sent care packages to him filled with ham, cake, apples, and books. At times she also sent money.

Charles Spurgeon also praised his mother, "I cannot tell you how much I owe to the solemn words of my mother." When he grew and started preaching, Charles and his mother wrote letters and encouraged one another. He praised her watchful eye during his childhood that protected him from making poor choices in friends and from using foul language, while guiding him to follow God's ways. Watching his mother through an illness, he marveled at her faith and cheerful attitude. Modeling her faith encouraged him as much as her words and impacted his own attitudes and preaching.

Today's Mom Step

Pray over your children aloud and call them by name as you ask for God to save them and protect them.

Letters to My Child

But encourage one another day after day, as long as it is still called "Today," so that none of you will be hardened by the deceitfulness of sin. HEBREWS 3:13

Kitty dropped another letter to her daughter in the mail. They'd talk later that day. It was hard to send her to the program for a few months, but she needed help. Anika had some PTSD from her childhood, before they adopted her, and needed more than one counseling session a week.

She wrote dog jokes in the card and words of encouragement.

That afternoon, Kitty found a letter from Anika in the mailbox. She read the jokes and the note about friends in the program and what they were doing. She opened a second note where Anika wrote an apology for some of the things she had done and also wrote, "I love you mom! You are so great. Keep writing. I like getting cards. I think I get the most mail. Grandma Terry and Grandma Connie send cards too."

After three weeks, Kitty and her husband visited Anika for an afternoon, the first time they saw her since she started the program. They hugged, and Kitty said, "I love your letters. They are on the fridge. Thanks for all the encouragement."

Anika thanked her mom and said she had some of the cards in her room. The counselors kept most of them in a box. Anika could look at them on days she finished all her tasks. Anika said, "Whatever animal is on the card, you write jokes about that type of animal. I want to keep my cards forever."

> **Today's Mom Step**
>
> Write words of encouragement to your children that they can hang up or keep in a special place.

Kitty smiled, "You catch on fast. We can pick out an album to hold your cards. I'm keeping my letters from you too."

Week 27

Bonding Blocks

Prayer to Build Lasting Relationships

Lord, help me build lasting bonds with my children. I want to remain close to them always. Help me invest time in them, show them my approval when they make good choices, discipline them with love, and rejoice in their joys.

Help my children know I accept each one as unique and created by you. Help my children know I love them unconditionally. Let them be close to one another and support and cheer each other.

Help us bond with extended family and friends to develop lasting connections. Help us grow strong together and support one another.

Let us spend time as a family celebrating, playing, talking, and working together. Guide me in what traditions to follow while creating great memories. Let us go through hardships together to grow stronger ties. Let our meals be a daily time of growth and conversation where we share our joys, laughter, and problems. Let each day add to building our bonds.

Wisdom from Future Moms

I think moms should favor everyone and not just a single one.

Mommy plays games and hunts. She dropped a clue from the laundry basket—a sock. I told her and she dropped more until she put the basket down. I gave her the clues and sorted clothes with her. Then she had the treasure for me, a snack! She's fun.

Starry Nights

Ah Lord GOD! Behold, You have made the heavens and the earth by Your great power and by Your outstretched arm! Nothing is too difficult for You. JEREMIAH 32:17

"Yay!! We get to stay up late. Dad's having a star gazing night."

The family headed outside, opened blankets and tossed down pillows. Mom brought out snacks to share later. They stood near the blankets as Dad pointed out constellations and a planet. The older children named some of the constellations.

No electricity due to the storm and a clear night sky made it easy to see many stars. Starlight and moonlight helped light up the yard. They found the big dipper, the little dipper, Virgo, Hercules, and Leo. Dad used his sextant with the older children to figure out different locations for these heavenly bodies.

They used the telescope to see the battered, rough surface of the moon, clusters of stars that were like pinpoints, and the nebulous clouds of gas that looked like snowflakes.

Then everyone lay on the blankets and stared up at the sky. Dad said, "Look! A falling star," and they all watched the shower of light falling through the air.

Dad talked about how God made the stars and how Psalms 147:4 reminds us that He named each ball of fire in the sky. He spoke about Job 38:31–32, where the twelve constellations are called the Mazzoreth.

Today's Mom Step

Enjoy a night of star gazing and praying as a family.

Then Dad said, "Your mom and I like to look out at the sky when we face problems and know God is watching over us and cares about our problems."

Mom said, "The twinkling stars give us hope that with God we can get through whatever happens. Even when we're apart we are all under the sky God made." They prayed together.

Inside the Womb (Biblical Mom, Proverbs Woman)

My frame was not hidden from You, when I was made in secret, and skillfully wrought in the depths of the earth. PSALMS *139:15*

You and your children all grew inside wombs with the loving care of God the Father. That's where bonds began with God and you. Adopted parents rejoice at the child they bring into the home and trust that their prayers for their child will be answered. God knit each child's DNA and every cell.

The joy of feeling the first movement within the womb and later seeing your child's movements strike a chord in our hearts and leave a memory. It's a joy to look at our child and watch this little one grow. As mothers, we start the relationship before we hold our child. We pray, hope, and dream of what will become. We build the relationship with prayer first as we reach out to God with the knowledge of the life on the way.

We prepare space for the child in the home. After the child's birth, we move forward with plans and add to them. Sometimes we manage from day to day, while other times we make special plans to celebrate a birthday, holiday, or special memory. Every plan and intentional action are another building block to develop strong bonds.

We are not perfect, and sometimes we hit a wall or fail to meet our own expectations or our child's expectations. Then we need to recall all the words of Psalm 139. God's eyes saw the unformed child you love. God made plans, too. God can search your heart. He created your child's heart. He ordained your days and the days of your child. We will face days of struggle and days we need repentance and forgiveness. Other days will be full of joy and peace. God will be with you and your child every day. Choose to bless your child and make each day count.

Skills for Life

So we built the wall and the whole wall was joined together to half its height, for the people had a mind to work. NEHEMIAH 4:6

PeggySue Wells used a chore system where each of her seven children had one weekly chore. It took about thirty minutes to make the home neat and functioning daily. So, if a chore was laundry, it had to be caught up and done before that chore could be handed off to the next kid the following week. If a chore was not done well, the child kept that chore for another week.

PeggySue taught worked alongside each child to show how to do it until they mastered it. A chore chart let the children take responsibility, so this mama did not remind or nag. One child had a chore he disliked for several weeks. He learned the fastest way to not have to do a task you don't like is to do it well and be able and turn it over to someone else. The little ones looked forward to getting their first chore of wiping the doorknobs with a wet cloth.

As the children became teens and adults, each of them called to thank their mother for enabling them to be self-sufficient. In job settings and at college they were usually the leaders who needed no supervision, did the work, noticed what needed to be done and did it. PeggySue said, "I got that phone call from my military son during a deployment."

He told her, "The captain called me into his office. Asked what I planned to do with my life. He said I am the only guy he's had on the destroyer who does whatever he asks and does it well the first time. Including cleaning the latrine. He said I could go anywhere with that attitude."

Today's Mom Step

Try teaching each chore and using a chore chart to raise responsible kids.

PeggySue thought of the time and attention and persistence she put into teaching them chores and guiding them to take full responsibility of what was in their hands to do. Their teamwork led to great life skills and a sense of family pride.

Quest for Freedom, Sojourner Truth (Historic Mom)

You will know the truth, and the truth will make you free. JOHN 8:32

In 1826, a six-foot tall woman named Sojourner escaped slavery in New York with her infant daughter Sophia. She became an advocate for other African American mothers. Born Isabella Baumfree, she changed her name, because she believed God led her on a journey to witness to the hope within her.

Sojourner experienced cruelty from her second owner who beat her regularly. She fell in love with a slave, but her owner forced her to marry a different slave. She gave birth to two sons and three daughters, although one son died in infancy. She found refuge with Isaac and Maria Van Wagenen who mentored her and later paid twenty dollars according to the New York anti-slavery law, to secure freedom for Sojourner. With the Van Wagenen's help she sued to gain custody of her son Peter, aged five, and won when she learned he had been sold and separated from the rest of his family. She became the first black woman to sue a white man in the U.S. and win.

She became a strong Christian and worked as a preacher's housekeeper. In 1843 she started preaching. In 1851 she spoke at an Ohio women's rights conference and gave her most famous speech called, "Ain't I a Woman?" She even met with President Abraham Lincoln. She rode on white-only streetcars in D.C. and helped find jobs for freed blacks. Peter took a job on a whaling ship, and they corresponded, but after some point she never heard from him again.

Today's Mom Step

As a mother and woman, follow God's call, for that's the greatest example for your children.

Sojourner eventually moved to Michigan to live near her daughters. She spoke out against discrimination. She said that the same God who made white skin also made black skin, so she was not to blame for her color and that God loves colored and white children.

A Stocking Tradition

O Ephraim, what more have I to do with idols? It is I who answer and look after you. I am like a luxuriant cypress; From Me comes your fruit. HOSEA 14:8

After reading the account of the birth of Jesus and singing "Happy Birthday," everyone grabbed their Christmas stockings and sat down. The youngest one started their stocking tradition.

Daniel pulled out an object and said, "A red car. My favorite color. God loves me. God made the colors of the rainbow."

Darlene took out batteries and said, "The Holy Spirit gives us power that lasts longer than batteries."

James pulled out an apple and said, "This is a fruit. The Holy Spirit gives us other fruit like joy and peace."

They continued around with mom and dad also sharing how items that filled the stocking reminded them of how God's love fills us, the Holy Spirit fills us, and how Jesus fulfilled prophecies to give us eternal life.

As they finished with the stockings, Darlene said, "Mom, opening stocking is my favorite Christmas tradition. It helps me think more about God."

James said, "We have lots of good traditions. I like when we decorate the tree. You read about God being like an evergreen tree. We talk about being part of our family and part of God's big family. Then we add lights to remember we are lights when we share our faith."

> **Today's Mom Step**
> Choose some family traditions that celebrate faith and build bonds.

Mom said, "I like the traditions too. They help us feel close to one another and to God. That's part of bonding that keeps us a happy and close family."

Week 28

Gratitude Alert

Prayer for Gratitude

Lord, help me be grateful for my blessings and thankful you are with me in my struggles. Let the sunrises and sunsets fill me with wonder and joy. Let the rain remind me you water the earth for new growth. When I start to complain, remind me to look for my blessings instead.

Help me be grateful when my children are sick that I am there to nurture them. When my children whine, let that be an alert to give them attention and a reminder of my own whining and need to appreciate what you give me. When my children fight, help me be patient and let it be an alert to cease my own anger and trust in you gratefully.

Like a siren blasting, let my own words of complaint be alerts that call me to pause, pray, and be loving.

As night descends let me pause and give thanks for the gift of children and family. Let me be thankful for the day even with its busyness and struggles for I have been blessed to be a mother.

Wisdom from Future Moms.

God gave me mom, 'cause she forgives easy, and He knew I need that a lot.

Mom prays for dad a lot. When his car drives in the garage, she says, "Thank God that daddy's home."

Mom-to-Mom Phone Calls

These things I have spoken to you so that My joy may be in you, and that your joy may be made full. JOHN 15:11

Casey answered the phone cringing a little as she knew Linda would start off with a cheerful greeting with her musical voice. They'd share their mom moments. Linda laughed at all their children's antics and rejoiced over their kind actions. Casey also had wonderful children and a great husband, but Linda's joy seemed artificial. They belonged to the same women's faith group and Linda had latched onto her. Their children got along well as did their husbands. Casey avoided Linda at meetings, but Linda always found her or saved her a seat and rushed up to claim her when she entered. Somehow Casey felt overwhelmed by all the positive chatter and giggles. Casey decided she had a bad attitude. She asked God to help her love Linda.

Slowly Casey started seeing how Linda's heart reached out to sprinkle joy in people's lives. She had the same sort of struggles as any mom but always responded with gratitude. Casey mentioned a few little gripes that troubled her and listened as Linda shared what she learned from those types of problems. Linda helped Casey change her attitude, and Linda seemed to realize Casey was not a morning person and responded better later in the morning or in the afternoons. They became great friends and felt so sad at parting when Casey moved away. The phone ringing became an alert that she could share joy too.

Linda's contagious joy moved Casey to call a woman when she felt the Holy Spirit

---

Today's Mom Step

Spread joy and call a friend when the Holy Spirit nudges you.

GROWING A MOTHER'S HEART

nudge her. She called that friend for a year; however, the gal seldom said much during their conversations. But one day the friend said, "Your calls meant so much. You often called when I was on the verge of tears and I could only listen. I needed those gratitude alerts."

Unexpected Miracle (Biblical Mom, Widow of Son Jesus Raised)

The dead man sat up and began to speak. And Jesus gave him back to his mother. LUKE 7:15

A widow's tears moved Jesus. He stood outside the gate of Nain, a name that means *pleasant*, There He saw a mother walking beside her dead son, about to be buried. He knew all about her. He knew the sorrow she'd face of burying her only son and the hardship that would follow with no one to support her, no more family to care for her. Only a few steps separated her present sadness from a bleak future.

The mourners' weeping and wailing would have made lots of noise and the parade of people would have filled the street. Jesus paused to speak to her and said, "Do not weep." He approached the casket and said to the dead man, "Young man, I say to you, arise." The man sat up and talked. Jesus gave him back to his mother. What an unexpected miracle and time for gratitude! The widow went from empty sorrow to embracing her beloved son. Widows with no family relied on charity when no jobs or social services meant poverty. She received new hope.

What a convergence of witnesses to the miracle! The disciples, the mourners, townspeople, and many people who followed Jesus as He traveled—they all stood amazed.

Great miracles seem rare, yet we have the joy as mothers of children healing from sickness and troubles being solved.

Little miracles and blessings are also wonderful and times to pause and be thankful. For mothers who lose a beloved child, it's comforting to know that Jesus feels such compassion. He calls mothers in sorrow to cease from crying and instead look to Him. Be grateful that Jesus is with us and we have someone who cares.

The people responded with gratitude. They said, "God has come to help His people."

Special Spiritual Care Packages

Whoever brings blessing will be enriched, and one who waters will himself be watered. PROVERBS 11:25 (ESV)

Karen felt burdened when her friend Patti cried out in grief at the murder of her son, a horrendous crime that left her with a grief-stricken six-year-old grandson Sammy, who lived with her, missing his uncle (and also his father-figure). Karen prayed and realized she could make a little care package for her friends, as she often did for various friends and children. She shopped at stores and found thirty little items for a care package. She picked up little toys that glowed or lit up, tops that twirled, snacks, colorful socks, balls, and little Bible storybooks. She found a scripture to match each item and wrapped it with the gift. On the outside, she added a note that posed a question or gave a humorous message. She gave the package to Patti.

Sammy enjoyed opening a little gift daily. He saved the papers, and they used them to chat about God and pray. He'd read the outside note and try to guess what he'd find inside. One note said, "God made animals that are fuzzy, helpful, and amazing." As he guessed, he found animals inside and a set of animal cards with the scripture Genesis 1:24 when God made animals.

Some of the items like a mustard seed story also talked about heaven with a note that his uncle he missed so much was in heaven. Patti could not stop hugging Karen after the first week of using the care package. She said it helped them be grateful and gave her words and thoughts to share with Sammy. With Sammy's mom on drugs and father not in the picture, Sammy had become very attached to his Grandma and uncle.

> **Today's Mom Step**
> Create a care package for a child who is struggling with loss, illness, or other problem.

Karen included a little more mention about heaven with each new care package, to help Sammy grieve, like a tiny notepad with a verse about rejoicing that our names are in God's book of life, so he could write his uncle's name and think about that.

Writer of Encouraging Words, Helen Steiner Rice (Historic Mom)

"Shout for joy, O barren one, you who have borne no child; Break forth into joyful shouting and cry aloud, you who have not travailed; For the sons of the desolate one will be more numerous than the sons of the married woman," says the Lord. ISAIAH 54:1

Helen Steiner Rice penned words that touched so many hearts but never had a child herself, Helen lost her father to the flu epidemic as a teen, and that ended her dreams of going to college.

Her husband died at age 32 to suicide, only one year into their marriage. Yet, she wrote about gratitude, love, and blessings for many decades.

People called her the Ambassador of Sunshine and America's Poet Laureate. As a girl, she loved writing rhymes and sharing God's love. When she started writing verses for Gibson Greeting Card Company, they wanted light, humorous verses for greeting cards—a perfect fit for Helen, because she believed people needed inspiration, and she often wrote those types of messages to friends and family. She finally approached her boss about using some of her inspirational verses on cards. When Lawrence Welk read her Christmas card on his program in 1960, it catapulted her to fame. She started speaking and writing more inspirational poems and books.

Today's Mom Step

Appreciate women in your life who do not have children but nurture many women anyway with a mother's heart.

Her poem, *A Mother's Love,* reflects the heart of a mother in all women. She expressed the unselfish love, sacrifice, and forgiving spirit of mothers that endures even when breaking. The words touch many mothers and continues to encourage them amid struggles they face.

Speaking from a heart that knew grief, Helen wrote about letting go and letting God lead the way. She remained close to many friends, family, and she treasured these relationships.

Basket Case Gratitude

Whatever you do in word or deed, do all in the name of the Lord Jesus, giving thanks through Him to God the Father. COLOSSIANS 3:17

Karen enjoyed making things, but life with a big family made that difficult. One day she grabbed a half-finished project and plopped everything in a basket. She intentionally left it by the door and took it with her to work on during her oldest son's soccer practices. Soon she had several baskets of various projects that each took differing amounts of time or focus.

Her family joined in with some of her basketry. One held a Christmas tree latch hook kit, and everyone worked on it during campouts. Needlepoint worked well during a daughter's dance lessons with tight seating. As she used her talents, she relaxed and prayed for the person who would receive the finished item. She thanked God for snatches of time to be creative.

Her children enjoyed trying to learn each type of handiwork, and she created projects for them too. Their baskets with covered fabric lids decorated the house and made good conversation starters. Each basket reminded Karen to be grateful for her talents and bits of creative time. They all celebrated the completion of any project, and dad considered it a mystery solved once he saw the results.

A Brazilian embroidery project of squares to make a quilt taking many years to complete hangs as a window treatment. Her older daughter claimed it as her heirloom since Karen worked on that when they spent time together. It's their gratitude quilt and a reminder that snatches of time add up.

Today's Mom Step

Indulge in a creative project that you can take on the go and be thankful for useful snatches of time.

Week 29

Seasoned Mothers

Prayer to Reach Out to Other Moms

Dear Lord, reading about ideal moms discourages me when I know you want to give me hope. In the dailiness of life I wonder how I can make it through to nightfall. I know you love me as I am and will guide me in whom I will become. You don't ask me to compare myself, yet when I meet a mom who seems to have it altogether, I begin to think about my shortcomings. Those seasoned moms should give me hope that I will improve and grow over time with experience. Help me welcome advice and aspire to improve and be like the woman in Proverbs 31.

As I grow, I am becoming seasoned. Let me rejoice in what I accomplish and what I learn. When my children see my imperfections and willingness to try again, that gives them hope and inspires them to try again when they fail.

Help me share with newer moms to impart a little of my experience. Each day I am called to simply nurture and care for my family's needs. Let me take that one day at a time.

Let me focus on what's most important and that's my faith and love. Help me be a loving mother and a faithful follower. Let love and faith be my guides as I make choices every day.

Wisdom from Future Moms

If I could change one thing about my mom, it would be for her to stop finding the mess under my bed.

My mommy is my hero.

Rebuilding Relationships

Great is his faithfulness; his mercies begin afresh each morning.
LAMENTATIONS *3:23 (NLT)*

Rebecca stopped by Brittany's job to say hello. She did this weekly in hopes of breaking down some walls. Brittany smiled, and Rebecca offered to drop off some diapers and things. Her daughter, adopted at seventeen, left home at eighteen, and now she was married with a little girl. At times she's spoke to Rebecca and at times she did not. Brittany wanted to make her own choices, and that included not finishing high school. Studying was too hard, and she had a poor memory.

Her offer opened some doors. On another day, Rebecca offered to drop off some extra stew when she cooked too much, and Brittany accepted the offer. Soon after, Brittany started asking for recipes and helping with cooking. She asked Rebecca to babysit at times. She and her family started going to church again with Rebecca and the rest of the family.

Brittany's husband started asking Brittany's dad for advice. He was also young and tried to find work he could do. Rebecca encouraged her younger daughter to bike over to talk and help with the baby. Before long, Brittany had a second child, this time amidst the COVID-19 pandemic. She called when she started feeling labor pains. Rebecca was in another city that day and gave them some advice on the phone. They had someone pick up their daughter as they were on their way to the ER, since the town had no hospital. She gave birth a few hours later to another little girl.

Today's Mom Step

Every day is a new opportunity to build bonds. Spend time today connecting with each child.

Rebecca's husband, a pastor, accepted a church position in another state, so they moved away but stayed in touch. Now they connect online to see the grandchildren. Brittany and her husband hope to move to be near them soon. They have all overcome lots of hurdles in rebuilding a relationship.

The Ideal Mom (Biblical Mom, Proverbs 31)

The heart of her husband trusts in her, and he will have no lack of gain. PROVERBS 31:11

Mother, wife, entrepreneur, community volunteer, and more. A mother wears many hats, and through the years of raising children we add to our abilities and accomplishments. We don't start at the finish line. There's a lot to learn and experience as mothers along our journeys.

The women described in Proverbs start with the heart and loyalty described in verse 11. Her husband's heart trusts in her. The passage ends with the phrase that "a woman who fears in the LORD . . . will be praised." Those are two key ideas. As we grow in faith, we become wiser and follow God more closely. As we grow in love and loyalty, we do what will benefit our loved ones and ourselves. We have what we really need if we have faith and remain loyal to our family.

It's a "one day, one season at a time" process. We transition many seasons from diaper days and tough toddler times to busy school days, trying tween and teen years, and then the empty-nester days, as our children emerge into adulthood. We share with those less experienced and glean from those more experienced. Most moms recall the seasoned moms who helped them along the way.

It takes a lifetime of mothering to do it all. This Proverbs 31 woman works with her hands whether cooking, creating, or hugging. She has strength and dignity, so she's built her mom muscles to protect her children and stand up against struggles. Throughout her life, she shops, nurtures her family, helps the needy, practices self-care, conducts business, and speaks with wisdom. It's not a dull life, and there's always room for new goals and new adventures.

Continue to seek out seasoned moms and be ready to be the seasoning for another mom who seeks your advice.

Jump Rope Team

For they disciplined us for a short time as seemed best to them, but He disciplines us for our good, so that we may share His holiness. HEBREWS 12:10

PeggySue Wells knew the importance of setting and keeping boundaries with her younger children. Her little girl adored being on the jump rope team, but she also avoided doing her schoolwork. PeggySue tried several ideas that had worked with the older children to get her to do the work, without success. One day, she simply let it go until her daughter said, "Mom it's time to go to jump rope practice."

PeggySue replied softly, "We're not going today."

"Why not?"

"Your schoolwork is not done. When it's done, I'll be delighted to take you." PeggySue remained calm and didn't remind her that's the rule. She knew her daughter knew the rules but chose to ignore them and other boundaries.

It only took that one time to make a difference. Her daughter kept up her work because she wanted to be on that team. A goal provides great motivation for a child. A boundary provides a great way for moms to enforce rules. The two found harmony with the balance of completed schoolwork and mom always ready to drive for jump rope practice and events. PeggySue loved watching her daughter, as did the siblings. She found more pleasure in applauding her daughter when she knew she saw her daughter's character develop.

Her daughter excelled in "double Dutch" and knew all the chants and songs to jump to, but she also knew her math tables. She jumped gracefully and with great enthusiasm but also increased her vocabulary and found she enjoyed reading and studying science.

> **Today's Mom Step**
> Maintain boundaries and rules and enforce the stated consequences calmly to alter behavior.

Jean Lowery, Steadfast Faith in Struggles (Historic Mom)

Jean, pregnant with her seventh child, clung to her faith after devastating circumstances in the early days of Pennsylvania. On April 1, 1756, Indians attacked, killed her husband, and captured her and five of her six children. She rebelled against her captives and refused to work on Sundays. One Indian tried to drown her but failed, so they gave her to a French commanding officer but kept her children. One of her sons shared her trust that God could deliver them out of captivity that reflected the faith in God she instilled in her little ones.

French soldiers moved her to Montreal and forced her to serve a French woman for a few years. Finally, a gentleman paid her passage to England, and strangers helped her return to Pennsylvania, where her uncaptured son maintained the family farm. She remarried and gave birth to another child. Throughout the next twenty-two years, she reunited with all of her children.

Early in her captivity Jean journaled, "The Lord sustained me. Glory to His name." Her faith helped her persist. She wrote her story and expressed distress at being separated from her children and not being able to teach them more of her faith.

> *I was now separated from all my Children, which was an inexpressible trouble unto me, for the Indians detained them all among them. Oh! how distressing to think that the fruit of my Body, and the delight of my Mind, as my Children were, that they should be brought up in Paganism, who were dedicated unto God and to be brought up in his fear and Service.*[2]

Today's Mom Step

Share faith today with your children, for we do not control the future.

A mother's nightmare with a happy ending gives us hope in the worst of times. Our greater hope remains in God and a future in heaven.

A Week's Break

Bear one another's burdens, and thereby fulfill the law of Christ. GALATIANS 6:2

Katya hugged her granddaughter Lea and said goodbye to her daughter. Lea would stay for one for a week to give her daughter a break. As a mom of five Katya knew sometimes a mom needs time off, especially if the child has various problems. Her adopted granddaughter struggled with learning problems and

---

2. http://tei.it.ox.ac.uk/tcp/Texts-HTML/free/N06/N06816.html

GROWING A MOTHER'S HEART

childhood trauma that left her with PTSD. This week they'd be sewing.

Lea wanted to make bandanas for their dogs. Katya taught her first how to make them without sewing. They used a cool glue gun too and also tried using bonding tape that melted pieces of fabric together with an iron. Then she taught Lea how to use a sewing machine. They practiced with scraps of fabric to make straight lines and sew close to the edge of fabric. Lea turned down edges and ironed them to form the hemlines and carefully sewed the hems. She made a dozen bandanas in various colors and patterns including one fabric with a dog bone print. Katya also scheduled fun activities and outings with her granddaughter, who lived nearby, to give Lea a break.

At home, Lea's mom took a break, spent time in prayer, and then reviewed Lea's schoolwork and her goals. She realized she was trying to get Lea to go faster than she could handle. She redid her schedule, found some online tools to help Lea practice math, and chose some hands-on activities to reinforce some of the concepts.

A week later mom and daughter happily reunited and returned to schoolwork refreshed.

> **Today's Mom Step**
> When you and your child are hitting a wall, try taking a break from one another or from the activity that causes tension.

Week 30

After Isn't Over

Prayer of a Forever Mom

Dear Lord, the journey through motherhood lasts for years as my children grow up. I discovered that at any age, I am still a mother, still on call for advice, empathy, and rejoicing, depending on the situation.

I realize mothering changes as children enter college or the job market and move out. Moms respond to calls, give advice, and have new worries about how they'll do on their own. As they marry, there's a new child, a bride or groom, to pray for, connect with, and build a new relationship. As my child becomes a parent, there's helping with grandchildren and reaching out for help as I age.

Give me the strength of endurance and persistence to never give up and never stop caring and praying for my children. Help me rejoice at each new stage and smoothly make the transitions as my child matures. Motherhood has always been full of changes with each age and stage of development with younger children. Help us continue the bonds all the days of our lives.

Wisdom from Future Moms

God made moms because he wants lots of kids in the world. He loves children.

I'll always be in her heart, and she'll always be in mine.

Nighttime Cry

You are from God, little children, and have overcome them; because greater is He who is in you than he who is in the world. 1 John 4:4

Eight-year-old Juliette's screams woke her mom. Mary raced in and realized her daughter had a fever. She'd had little energy lately and looked pale. Moments later, Juliette threw up and then passed out. Mary called 911. Mary tried to lift Juliette up, but she was too floppy and hit her head on the toilet.

The ambulance came. Only one person was allowed to go to the hospital due to COVID-19, so Mary and Juliette went to the hospital while her husband and teen son stayed home and cried. The doctors examined Juliette, said it could be a few possibilities, and asked Mary what condition she suspected. She replied, "It's leukemia."

The doctors confirmed it. However, the good news is that Juliette's form of leukemia has a 99% rate of healing with treatment. Juliette's pediatrician called Mary in the ER and said they faced a long, hard journey. She and Gary had to switch off being at the hospital, with rules only allowing a switch once every five days.

The first two months included pneumonia and lots of doctor visits. Juliette was always a joyful child, and the nurses and medical staff all enjoyed her sense of humor and smile. All the cards and gifts sent kept up everyone's spirits. Thankfully, after two months she perked up and swam, played tennis with her older brother, and enjoyed her crafts. With one teen already, Mary thought she'd been seasoned enough, but cancer

---

Today's Mom Step

Be thankful for professionals who help in times of need.

---

brought on a whole new set of challenges, especially during the COVID-19 quarantine.

Mary has gained a new appreciation for the kindness and expertise of medical workers. Juliette loves her child life specialists who are always available and know all her favorite games, shows, and books. Juliette can hardly wait to ring the bell when her cancer treatments end.

Mary, a Hospitable Mom
(Biblical Mom, Mary, Mother of John Mark)

And when he realized this, he went to the house of Mary, the mother of John who was also called Mark, where many were gathered together and were praying. Acts 12:12

Children know what homes welcome them with open doors. When an angel released the chains for Peter and led him out to the street to freedom and left him standing there, Peter made a quick decision. He headed to the home of Mary, the mother of John (also called Mark or John Mark). He knew where to find friends and hospitality. He knew people gathered at Mary's house in Jerusalem to pray.

Peter knocked. The servant girl Rhoda heard the knock and felt joy at hearing Peter's voice, but she didn't open the door. Rhoda announced that Peter stood at the gate. They didn't believe her until they heard Peter continue to knock. Finally, someone opened the door and Peter explained the miracle of the angel. Then Peter left.

Moms who have open doors let people come and go without lots of questions. They make visitors feel comfortable but don't try to hold them back from their plans and goals. Mary and her son also knew Paul well. He came after Peter, along with John

Mark's cousin Barnabas, and took John Mark with them on a mission trip to Antioch.

Today's Mom Step

Pray for your children and all the friends they bring into your home and ask each visitor how you can pray for him or her.

John Mark wrote the Gospel of Mark and traveled as a missionary. His mother saw her son embrace faith as his own. She and others probably continued praying for her son and the other believers, especially the ones who went on trips to spread the good news. Her role as a mother extended to caring for all those who entered her home. Her revolving door kept things busy as it became known as a hub and prayer stop for missionaries.

Distance Help

As each one has received a special gift, employ it in serving one another as good stewards of the manifold grace of God. 1 PETER 4:10

Susan called her daughter often. Kim homeschooled and needed to bounce off ideas, get sympathy on rough days, and sometimes ask for advice. Susan had homeschooled Kim and her other children so she could share from experience.

Kim set up online calls so the children could read to their grandma and share the reports they wrote with her. That eased some of the teaching duties for Kim. Five children kept Kim very busy.

Once a year, Susan drove hours to stay a week or two with Kim. She let Kim continue teaching while she organized things and did some deep house cleaning. That helped a lot too.

Kim called, "Mom, it's hard to keep up some days. I know Anja would like to do more crafts, but I don't have time."

Susan replied, "I can send some supplies and then share ideas online with her." Kim said, "I love how you understand because you've been in my shoes." Susan began doing some art lessons and then knitting lessons with Anja and then the others who asked for art with grandma.

Susan's doorbell rang, and she opened it to a delivery person with a basket of goodies. Her grandchildren had sent a thank you with treats, a knitted hat, and some framed artwork.

She asked for a Zoom® meeting and said, "You made

> **Today's Mom Step**
> Give yourself a break with letting an extended family member do online activities with your children, so they can share their experience and talent.

my week with your gifts! I displayed all the handcrafted items. It's like an art show at my house. Thanks for sharing your talent." She walked around to let her camera show where she placed each piece sent.

Queen Victoria, Mother and Leader (Historic Mom)

Queen Victoria knew her success was rooted in faith. When an African prince asked what brought success to the British Empire, she handed him a copy of the Bible and said, "This book."

She gave birth to nine children with her husband Prince Albert. She suffered postpartum depression after a number of the births. Her role as queen kept her from being involved in the daily lives of her children, but her husband took a much more active parental role until his death. As they grew, Victoria kept in touch through letters. She wrote many letters and kept a diary. She filled her diary with the reasons she disliked children due to noise and such. But she filled her letters to friends with the delights of her children. The contrasting thoughts reveal how many mothers know they love their children but also struggle with the little behaviors that annoy them.

Victoria's talk about problems of pregnancy, breastfeeding, and newborns brought such problems into public discussion.

As a widow, Victoria wanted her youngest child Beatrice to remain close to her. Except for her brief marriage that ended when her husband died, Beatrice stayed by her mother's side as a friend and secretary.

Victoria mourned the loss of her husband for the remainder of her life. They had remained deeply in love for their twenty-one years of marriage. Although considered a controversial mother, she exerted great influence over her children and her grandchildren. Most of Queen Victoria's children married royalty. Queen Elizabeth II is a descendant of Victoria and has held great influence in the world. A determined woman, Victoria always revealed her optimistic heart and led her people during a time of changes in industry, politics, science, and culture.

> **Today's Mom Step**
>
> Today's words and choices will be part of the legacy your leave your children, so choose wisely.

After Isn't Over

And after you have suffered for a little while, the God of all grace, who called you to His eternal glory in Christ, will Himself perfect, confirm, strengthen, and establish you. 1 PETER 5:10

Karen's son, Michael played with his friend one afternoon. As the time drew near for his friend to leave, she announced, "Boys, it's time to clean up. Ben will be leaving in thirty minutes."

Michael pleaded with his mom to let him keep out the toys. "I promise to clean it all up by himself after Ben leaves." She agreed, knowing it provided an opportunity for her son to show responsibility.

Ben left, and two hours later Karen returned to the play area to see the toys scattered on the floor and Michael playing. She asked, "Michael, you promised to clean up. Why is everything still out?"

Michael looked up with his big blue eyes and quietly said, "Mom, after isn't over yet."

She laughed, thinking how her son and she viewed time differently. She said to her son, "After just ended." He began picking up his toys. Then she considered how God views time differently, too.

We pray and expect God to respond immediately. He gently reminds us that our prayer time isn't over and to keep praying. He wants us to persist. In difficult trials we ask God to end the pain and get us through it quickly. He responds that He will do it in His perfect time, after we've learned what He needs to teach us. We think, as soon as they potty train, or start the next level of school, or move out, this phase of mothering will end. We look for ends, but God shows us new beginnings. Moms always encounter new aspects in parenting. And after is never over for moms. Our children will always be in our hearts.

> **Today's Mom Step**
> Embrace today's mom moments.

Contributors

BETH BRUBAKER's passion is the written word. She shares her brand of humor with the world through poems, songs, and stories. She enjoys sharing her struggles and experiences while encouraging others to find their own passions and attain what they want out of life—and to find joy and humor along the way.

Thirteen-year-old ISABELLA THEODORA CARDWELL, from Virginia, dedicated her restored life to helping people praise the Lord. She writes, sketches, paints, and composes songs and piano music. Her first book is *Let All the Earth Praise*. She shares her testimony of her slow healing journey that began with her prayer, "Use me however you can, as broken as I am."

PAM FARREL is an international speaker, Co-Director of Love-Wise with her husband, Bill, award-winning author of fifty plus books including the bestselling *Men Are Like Waffles, Women Are Like Spaghetti; 10 Best Decisions a Parent Can Make, Discovering Hope in the Psalms* and *Discovering Joy in Philippians*. She is mom to three sons and daughter in laws, and five grands.

In her adult life, SANDRA FELTON was a disorganized wife and mom with three kids and a fulltime job, plus a chronically messy house. Desperately seeking relief from clutter, she sought help from information in books and from friends. She found the "secrets" that finally worked for her and shared her valuable insights in a series of helpful books about household organizing.

Authentic. Passionate. Funny. All describe BECKY HARLING. A best-selling author, Becky is a popular speaker at conferences, and other events. She has been a guest on many radio and TV shows. Becky holds a degree in biblical literature and is a certified leadership and communications coach.

LINDA EVANS SHEPHERD is a speaker and bestselling author of over thirty-six books including *Praying Through Your Every Emotion*, *Praying God's Promises*, and *When You Need to Move a Mountain*. She founded Right to the Heart Ministries, Arise Esther, the Advanced Writers and Speakers Association (AWSA), *Leading Hearts* Magazine, and the *ARISE* Daily Devotional.

CYNTHIA L. SIMMONS is the mother of five grown children, past president of Christian Authors Guild, radio host, media coach, and columnist for *Leading Hearts* magazine. She writes both fiction and nonfiction and loves history. She has a special place in her heart for young mothers and homeschool mothers. (https://clsimmons.com)

YVONNE ORTEGA speaks with honesty and humor as she shares her life and struggles to help women find peace and purpose in life's challenges. She's been interviewed multiple times for her Moving from Broken to Beautiful® Book Series. She celebrates life at the beach, where she walks, blows bubbles, builds sandcastles, and dances.

JULIETTE WALSH is a 3rd grader. She's eight and a half, funny, smart, kind, and generous. She likes Irish step dancing and playing basketball with her brother.

History buff and tropical island votary, PEGGYSUE WELLS parasails, skydives, snorkels, scuba dives, and has taken (but not passed) pilot training. The solo mom of seven and former radio show host is the bestselling author of twenty-nine books including The What To Do series, *The Slave Across the Street*, *Bonding with Your Child through Boundaries*, *Homeless for the Holidays*, and *Chasing Sunrise*.

Drawing from her walk with Christ and decades as a Christian counselor and Bible teacher, DEBBIE W. WILSON helps women enjoy grace-filled lives. Her most recent book *Little Faith, Big God* explores the lives and lessons found in Hebrews 11. Find free resources and connect with Debbie at debbieWwilson.com.

When you purchase a Bible or book from **AMG Publishers, Living Ink Books,** or **God and Country Press,** you are helping to impact the world for Christ.

How? AMG Publishers and its imprints are ministries of **AMG International,** a Gospel-first global ministry that meets the deepest needs – spiritual and physical – while inspiring hope, restoring lives and transforming communities. Profits from the sale of AMG Publishers' books are poured into AMG International's worldwide ministry efforts.

For over 75 years, AMG International has leveraged the insights of local leaders and churches, who know their communities best to identify the right strategies to meet the deepest needs. AMG's methods include child and youth development, media evangelism, pastor training, church planting, medical care and disaster relief.

To learn more about AMG International and how you can partner with the ministry through your prayers and financial support, please visit **www.amginternational.org**.

AMG INTERNATIONAL | MEETING THE DEEPEST NEEDS